The Supporting Cast

A COMEDY IN TWO ACTS

by George Furth

D1178545

SAMUEL FRENCH, INC.
45 WEST 25TH STREET   NEW YORK 10010
7623 SUNSET BOULEVARD   HOLLYWOOD 90046
LONDON   *TORONTO*

FOR DEMMY

Opening Night Sunday, February 14

THE SOUTHERN CALIFORNIA THEATRE ASSOCIATION

presents the

JAMES A. DOOLITTLE PRODUCTION

of

BARBARA RUSH   MARCIA RODD   JOYCE VAN PATTEN

CAROLE COOK   GEORGE FURTH

in

THE SUPPORTING CAST

a new comedy by

GEORGE FURTH

Scenery and Lighting by

GERRY HARITON and VICKI BARAL

Costume Coordinator

WILLIAM WARE THEISS

Directed by

TOM TROUPE

Opening Night August 7, 1981

BILTMORE THEATRE
UNDER THE DIRECTION OF THE MESSRS. NEDERLANDER

Terry Allen Kramer, James M. Nederlander and
Twentieth Century Fox
present

SANDY
HOPE DENNIS JACK
LANGE   GILFORD

BETTY   JOYCE
GARRETT   VAN PATTEN

in

THE SUPPORTING CAST

a new comedy by

GEORGE FURTH

Scenery by   Costumes by   Lighting by
William Ritman   Jane Greenwood   Richard Nelson

Directed by

GENE SAKS

"Life, [etc.] . . . are battlefields
which have their heroes; obscure
heroes, sometimes greater than
the illustrious heroes."

Victor Hugo
Marius
Book V, Chapter 1

5

CAST

Ellen . . . . HOPE LANGE

Mae . . . . BETTY GARRETT

Sally . . . . SANDY DENNIS

Arnold . . . . JACK GILFORD

Florrie . . . . JOYCE VAN PATTEN

TIME
The Present

PLACE
A beach house in Malibu, California

THERE WILL BE ONE INTERMISSION

STANDBYS
Standbys never substitute for listed players unless specific notification
is made at the time of performance.

For Mae and Florrie—Chevi Colton; For Ellen and Sally—Claiborne Cary

LA CAST
(in order of appearance)

ELLEN . . . . *Barbara Rush*
MAE . . . . *Carole Cook*
SALLY . . . . *Marcia Rodd*
ARNOLD . . . . *George Furth*
FLORRIE . . . . *Joyce Van Patten*

STANDBYS
Standbys never substitute for listed players unless a specific notification
is made at the time of performance.

For Ellen and Florrie—Jennifer Rhodes
For Mae and Sally—Patricia Smith

The Supporting Cast

ACT ONE

TIME: *Late November. This year.*

PLACE: *Malibu, California.*

SETTING: *Onstage, we see the deck of a beach house overlooking the Pacific Ocean. The deck is rectangular, warm, elegant and comfortable. Large pillows on the outdoor sofas and chairs. Wide board planks make up the floor. A large coffee table stands in front of the sofa and two small tables are either side of the stage. A bar is Downstage L.*

There are hanging ferns and plants scattered around in handsome containers.

Upstage L. is a round dining table, which will be used to put food on for the luncheon, and chairs.

Offstage we see, through a large serving window Downstage L., the kitchen. The window slides open and closed and is now closed. There is a shelf running along the outdoor length of it for putting out food. There is an upper balcony Upstage L. and a glass sliding door open out onto it.

Sliding glass doors Upstage C. reveal the inside living room . . . we can see white carpeting and furniture, a fireplace, paintings, plants, etc.

NOTE: In order to avoid a lighting problem with the glass in the doors and windows it is suggested that the aluminum door frames have a rim of 1½ or 2 or so inches of plexiglass with a line of silver stipping across the inner edge. The silver stipping cre-

ates an illusion that it is a fully glassed door with a common burglar alarm system. A kick plate should be placed on the bottom edge of the door so the actors can bump it creating the sound of colliding with a glass door. It is further suggested that the windows be made by using only the aluminum sliding frames with no glass at all. Actors are warned when the doors and windows are closed no sound should be heard from the living room or kitchen areas inside the house.

If production is done in the round it is suggested a firmly anchored sliding glass door be on stage separating the small area living room and the large area deck. If there is an orchestra pit use that area for the kitchen with a simple balcony built over it.

ELLEN, the hostess is very good-looking. She is generally bright, alive, ever optimistic and happy . . . but there is something very tense and nervous going on with her today. And SHE is working much too hard to conceal it. Her hair, clothes and makeup all look carelessly wonderful, yet great care always goes into all three. From the moment we see her it will become apparent today is the most urgently important day of her life.

MRS. MAE RISIAN is an energized, feisty, attractive woman, enthusiastic about everything and everyone. It is almost an over-reaction except for its sincerity. SHE is simply expansive and quite pretty.

SALLY appears very eastern seaboard, wears tinted sunglasses, many soft layers of clothes, sandals, her hair in a Gibson-girlish sweep. SHE carries a scarf, often putting it around her neck, waist, head or just carrying it and pulling at it. SHE demands ceaseless

attention and sympathy, and speaks from an almost
tragic and hurt place that seems oddly humorous,
probably from the fact that in unguarded moments
it is clear SHE *is strong as a bull.*

ELLEN. (*Offstage.*) Mae, Sally. (ELLEN *appears on*
the upper balcony, opening the door.) Come out here
and see why they call it the Pacific. (ELLEN *picks up a*
hockey stick, sneakers and football jersey up there and
holds them.)

MAE. (*Enters, looking out.*) We've got one of those in
New York. We call it the Hudson. It's fabulous.

ELLEN. (*Calling.*) Sally, do you want to come out on
the deck?

SALLY. (*Entering, looking down.*) I hate heights.

ELLEN. It's not really high.

SALLY. (*Looking out.*) If it's off the ground I hate it.

ELLEN. Will you two just look at that ocean.

SALLY. I'm allergic to water.

ELLEN. (*Exiting.*) Come on, let me show you both the
downstairs.

MAE. (*Following* ELLEN *exiting.*) It's a beautiful
house, Ellen. Beautiful. (*Turns back to* SALLY.) Could
you live like this? I'd kill myself.

(MAE *exits.* SALLY, *alone on the upper deck, in a*
panic inches herself into the house and closes the
door. We see ELLEN *coming down the stairs and*
crossing the living room where SHE *sees a man's*
sweater on the chair there. SHE *picks it up and then*
holds it to her, upset. At that second MAE *enters the*
living room and ELLEN *exits Offstage* L. *As* MAE

looks around in the kitchen SALLY *comes down the steps into living room and as* SHE *goes to take a step out onto the deck with a large bang* SHE *bumps into the glass door. Amazed,* SHE *slides open the door and walks out onto the deck massaging her breast which* SHE *just hit.*)

MAE. (*Continued.*) (*Having missed all that joins* SALLY *and* THEY *look at the ocean.*) See, all this Malibu is remarkable to me. I live in New York.

SALLY. I do too.

MAE. Whereabouts?

SALLY. The east side.

MAE. Oh, really? (*Looks her up and down. Then crossing Far Up* R. *to look over the property.*) I carry a picture of the east side around in my wallet. (*Gives her a dirty look and exits through the Upstage* R. *high garden gate.*)

ELLEN. (*Entering.*) What did I miss?

SALLY. Ellen, do you know my whole apartment could fit into your living room. I'd hate to ask you what a house like this is worth. (SALLY *crosses back into the living room and out of sight as* MAE *walks back from Upstage* R. *fence not having heard* SALLY.)

MAE. What is a place like this worth?

ELLEN. What do you guess?

MAE. A fortune.

ELLEN. More. And it's very comforting to know you can always sell your house and buy Battle Creek, Michigan. (ELLEN *puts her arm around* MAE *and* THEY *walk Stage* L.) Oh, Mae, I was hoping you'd get here first. I'm just beside myself today and I have to tell *some*body. I am just frantic.

MAE. Her?

ELLEN. No.

MAE. Me?

ELLEN. No.

MAE. Your book?

ELLEN. Yes. Well, in a way.

MAE. What do you mean 'in a way'.

ELLEN. (THEY *sit at table* L.) Oh Mae, you know as well as I know the kind of book people would expect a person like me to write. Well, I have not written a children's book and I have not written a cookbook. I have written a book about people and the people I have written about are coming here today.

MAE. And they don't know they're in this book.

ELLEN. And they don't know they're in this book. Oh, Mae, I was planning to tell them one by one. Not fake this luncheon and bully them out here like this.

MAE. Oh, Ellen, that's awful.

ELLEN. No, no, here's the awful part. The book is done, it's printed, it's ready for shipment. My God, I've got these contracts around all over the place. But now the publisher has stopped everything until I get *waivers* signed by everyone I based a character on.

MAE. Do you mean it's that easy to tell who they are?

ELLEN. No. It's not at all. And the book is fiction. But suddenly there are so many lawsuits these days against this kind of fiction, that are actually being won, that unless I get the waivers signed the publishers are simply cancelling the book. So it won't come out at all, you see?

MAE. Yes, I see. You've buried your friends.

ELLEN. No, of course not, they'll love it. At least I always assumed they'd love it.

MAE. Then what is the problem?

ELLEN. John read the book and had a terrible reaction and now I'm panicked. That's the reason I invited all—

SALLY. (*Interrupting, entering from gate Upstage* R.) Now what did I miss? (*Crosses Downstage to chair* R.)

MAE. (*Gets up from table and crosses to sofa and sits.*) I was just admiring this house. You can tell when a person's real rich because they have no antiques.

ELLEN. You will notice that I am closing the doors. (*Closing the glass door and crossing to them, stopping between sofa and chair* L.) I'm insane about keeping the doors and the windows closed because anything nice just gets ruined by that ocean air. Oh God. Oh, is that beach not something?

SALLY. (*Sitting in chair* R.) Sand works as an irritant on my skin.

MAE. Am I crazy or do I smell smoke?

SALLY. Oh, thank God someone else smells it. I am simply fighting for air.

ELLEN. (*Sits on* R. *cushion of sofa next to* MAE.) That's from that fire in the hills. It's a mile up the road. That's another reason I'm keeping the doors and windows closed.

MAE. That's not that same fire that's been burning for over a week?

ELLEN. It's just that time of year out here. Every October, November. Listen, would you both rather go inside?

SALLY. Absolutely not. I'd much prefer choking to death to burning to death.

ELLEN. Good. Because when the other two get here we're eating outside. Oh, Mae, will you look at this day.

SALLY. Am I the only one who's cold?

ELLEN. Sally, you want a sweater? We have tons.

SALLY. No, maybe it's just me. (*To* MAE.) Excuse me. Excuse me. Aren't you at all cold?

MAE. No, I'm fine. (SHE *knocks on wood.*)

ELLEN. Sally, this is a perfect day.

SALLY. Oh, how I envy people who have hides like cattle.

ELLEN. (*Crosses behind sofa to exit.*) Listen, let me run inside and steal a sweater. Does anyone want anything else?

MAE. (*Stopping her.*) Yes, *I* want to know where's John? Where are the kids?

ELLEN. They send their love.

SALLY. (*Angry. Turning her head away.*) Oh, dear merciful God in heaven. (*Turning to* MAE.) Where do you think they are?

MAE. Where?

SALLY. On that endless tour of that endless house her children and her husband were not mentioned once. (*Almost yells at her.*) Get it?

ELLEN. (*Crosses between sofa and chair* L.) No, Sally, no, no. The boys are at college and John is working. (*Picks up basketball under coffee table.*) As a matter of fact this basketball is John's. Before he even comes in every night he spends about fifteen minutes out there shooting baskets. (*She throws basketball over the fence and crosses back checking watch. Stands behind sofa.*) Isn't it funny that the other two aren't here yet?

SALLY. That's not nearly as funny to me as a person who spends over a year writing a book and hasn't said a word about it. Is it a children's book, a cookbook? (ELLEN *pokes* MAE.) Is it filthy?

ELLEN. I just don't want to talk about it *yet.*

SALLY. Oh God, it's like the Pentagon papers. (ELLEN *crosses Downstage* L. *and puts flowers from window ledge on floor next to bar.*) Could we please just drop it?

SALLY. How are you going to display it in bookstores?

In plain brown paper wrappers?

ELLEN. (*Behind bar wiping hands, laughing.*) Thank you for dropping it.

MAE. Well, we know it's going to be genius because the last time Ellen went into hiding for a year was when she helped John write "The Graying of the White House." I hope you got half that Pulitzer Prize for that book.

ELLEN. Well first of all I'm not a genius and second of all I didn't help him write it. You want to know what I did while John was writing that book? I kept the telephone off the hook and the house quiet so he could think. (ELLEN *crosses up to sliding glass door.*)

MAE. John said you did more than half of the research and all of the typing and everything. (ELLEN *slides open door.*)

ELLEN. Oh, did I leave that out. He's absolutely right.

MAE. Where is he?

ELLEN. I told you. Working. (SHE *slides closed the glass door and, exiting, crosses into the kitchen where we see her force relaxation and pour a glass of wine and take a quick drink.*)

SALLY. That marriage is over.

MAE. Over?

SALLY. Finished, through, forget it. I bet you whoever we're waiting for is her lover. Yes. I will be able to tell as soon as he comes in. So when he comes in look at me and (*Indicates up and down then side to side with her hand and head.*) I'll shake my head "yes" or "no" if I think it's her lover.

MAE. To think Ellen, the one everybody comes to with their problems, is suddenly the one whose got the prob—

(ELLEN *slides open the glass doors near the end of*

that, entering, and MAE *and* SALLY, *almost caught, change totally.* ELLEN, *carrying a sweater, crosses to* SALLY *and gives it to her.*)

MAE & SALLY. (*Together.*) Hi.

ELLEN. Hi. I'm so glad you two are getting to know each other. Here you go, Sally. Anybody want anything else? (ELLEN *crosses to bar.*)

MAE. No, I'm just fine.

SALLY. (*Stands, crossing between sofa* R. *and coffee table.*) Do you have any aspirin?

ELLEN. Sally, aspirin's very bad for your system.

SALLY. So are headaches. I would like some aspirin.

MAE. Did you go to the bathroom today?

SALLY. (*Startled.*) Yes. (ELLEN *getting the aspirin bottle and glass of water.*)

MAE. There goes that theory.

ELLEN. Sally? How many do you want?

SALLY. (*Takes aspirin bottle from* ELLEN *and sits on sofa* R. *cushion.*) Six.

ELLEN. You take six and you won't even have a system. (*Gives water to* SALLY *and sits on arm of Downstage* R. *chair.*)

SALLY. Despite my looks I am over twenty one. I'm only going to take two right now. (SALLY *puts four aspirin in her pocket and swallows two.*)

ELLEN. Is it a bad headache?

SALLY. No, Ellen, it's a good headache. I feel like I am right on the edge of the most enormous anxiety attack.

MAE. (*Reaches for purse.*) I've got some Valium if you want.

SALLY. (*Interrupting.*) Valium! You don't! I'm so relieved you have Valium. How many do you have?

MAE. (*Has found them. Is counting.*) Uh, three.

SALLY. (*Taking them all.*) Perfect. (*Swallows one and*

puts the other two in her pocket.)

ELLEN. (*Crossing to bar and begins making Bloody Marys.*) It's better living through chemistry.

MAE. (*Putting empty bottle into her purse and taking out her hand mirror and looking in it.*) I've been in the habit of taking one when I fly. Thanks for helping me break the habit.

SALLY. (*Take the hand mirror from MAE.*) Oh, God. I am going to have everything I have two of lifted. Who else is coming? (*Gives mirror back to MAE.*)

ELLEN. Just two more. I've got Bloody Marys on the way and I've got wine—

MAE. (*Trying to see her lapel watch.*) What time is it? I never drink until it's officially noon.

ELLEN. It's after one, Mae.

MAE. Then double the vodka. (*SALLY has taken a paper bag out of her pocket and has begun breathing into the bag as MAE watches. Then.*) Listen, uh . . . I just totally forgot your name. Isn't that terrible? What is it?

SALLY. Sally. (*Still holding her chest.*)

MAE. And it suits you. Usually I jump right in and say, "Oh, I knew *that*, it's your *last* name I forgot," but life is short and what the hell. Anyway, Sally, I don't mean to be impertinent, but is something bothering you that you'd like to get off your chest? Or not. It's up to you. (*SALLY goes back to chair Downstage R.*)

ELLEN. Sally is going through a divorce.

SALLY. (*Sits in chair Downstage R.*) Divorce! It is most certainly not a divorce. There has not been one word said about a divorce. In fact, I have not seen nor heard from him since that thing with the car.

ELLEN. What thing with the car?

SALLY. I told you about the car.

ELLEN. No, you didn't tell me anything about a car.

SALLY. I told you about the car. The brand new silver Mercedes. When he phoned me out here to tell me that car which I drove here from New York was *his* car, in *his* name, and he was sending me his power of attorney to sell it and send him the money. So I sold the car for fifty dollars and sent him the money.

MAE. I assume you're not planning on getting back together with your husband.

SALLY. As far as I'm concerned I am not even separated.

MAE. You might be more separated than you think.

ELLEN. Well, you can't dwell on things that are done. You can't. Just like I can't dwell on someone not liking my book. (*Crosses to* MAE *with tray with three Bloody Marys and* MAE *takes one.*)

SALLY. Who didn't like your book?

ELLEN. (*Crossing around coffee table serving* SALLY *from the tray, then sits on couch next to* MAE. ELLEN *takes the last Bloody Mary.*) What?

SALLY. I said who didn't like you book?

ELLEN. Oh, did I say that?

MAE. I think she just used that as an example.

ELLEN. I did. Yes, I did. And a divorce is nobody else's business anyway.

SALLY. I am not going through a divorce!

ELLEN. I don't know why I said "divorce."

SALLY. He doesn't even speak to me much less ask me for a divorce. If he wants a divorce let him ask me for a divorce then I will never *give* him a divorce. That sick tramp he's living with wants his name that's all. Oh, he just loved that I used to be as neurotic as she is. And he just couldn't deal with it after I got well. (SHE *gets up and crosses to the bar where* SHE *pours her glass of water back into the water pitcher.*) Oh, I'm on to her. She's only after him because of who he is.

MAE. Who the hell is he?

ELLEN. Sally was married to Geroge Stern. Congressman Stern. (SALLY *moves phone from behind bar to small phone table Downstage* R.)

SALLY. *Is* married, not *was* married.

ELLEN. *Is* married.

MAE. Oh, *that's* who you are.

ELLEN. That's who she is. (SALLY *crosses around the Stage* L. *dining table trying to still her anxiety, squatting and standing and doing deep breathing.*) Actually, that is the least part of her. Sally is this wonderfully giving, kind, funny—mess, is what she is right now. (SALLY *has knelt in front of phone table and picked up the phone receiver.*) Uh, Sally—who are you calling?

SALLY. (*Puts the receiver back down.*) I don't know. Him. Isn't that insane. Because there is no way to call him. He has all these codes. (*Puts phone back under the bar, then fills her water glass with vodka.*) Ring three times, hang up, ring back twice, hang up and then ring back. (*She holds up her index finger.*) This finger is one inch shorter than all the rest (*Holds middle finger up next to index finger.*) just from dialing my husband. (SALLY *puts filled glass of vodka on dining room table* L. *and crosses behind sofa looking for her purse.*)

ELLEN. (*Crossing Up to the bar to make another pitcher of Bloody Marys.* ELLEN *moves* SALLY'S *glass from dining table to bar to stop her from drinking more.*) I think I'll make some more Bloody Marys. For the *others*. To throw at them.

MAE. A lot of people say George Stern could be President some day. (SALLY, *crossing behind* MAE, *raises her hands indicating* SHE'D *like to strangle* MAE *and then continues looking for her purse.*) Ellen, you always could make a fabulous Bloody Mary.

ELLEN. I would tell you the secret is horseradish if it weren't such a puny secret.

SALLY. (*Very bothered by what* MAE *said,* SHE *now is crossing to the sliding doors.*) Excuse me. Excuse me, I want to get my muscle relaxants. I left them in my purse. (*And* SHE *walks right into the glass door. Stunned,* SHE *turns, looks at them a long second then falls to her knees.*)

ELLEN. (*Hurrying to her with* MAE, *helping her up.*) Now is that the craziest thing?

MAE. Oh, my goodness. What did you hit?

SALLY. (*As* THEY *help her to sofa, holding her knee, furious.*) None of your business. (MAE *moves quickly away, above sofa.*) I *know* he could be President.

ELLEN. (*Helping* SALLY.) Here. Let me. Oh, Sally, did you hurt yourself?

SALLY. (*Sitting on sofa* L.) No, it was wonderful, Ellen, I loved it. Oh, how I hate this day (*Rubbing her knee.*)

MAE. Sally, precious, let me run and get your purse with the relaxants. I'll be right back. In a jiff. (*As* SALLY *moans* MAE *turns and runs right into the glass sliding door.*)

ELLEN. (*Going Up to* MAE.) Why *suddenly* can no one see it's a door? Where did you hit?

MAE. (*Holding the bridge of her nose.*) It's fine. I always thought it should be bigger anyway.

(ELLEN *slides open and then after* MAE *exits,* ELLEN *slides closed the glass door . . .* MAE *exits into the living room and Off* L.)

ELLEN. This has never happened. Never. Not once to anyone before today. (*Crossing back to* SALLY.) Sally, where did you hit?

SALLY. Is there a lump?

ELLEN. Take your hand away. (SALLY *shows her knee.*) Yes.

SALLY. Where? (ELLEN *places* SALLY'S *hand on the lump.*) Oh, that lump has been there. That's from when I rode my tricycle down the front steps.

ELLEN. When?

SALLY. When? Yesterday, when. I hate looking at my legs anyway. Why is it the knees always go first? Is there another lump? I'll look like I have my ass on my knee.

ELLEN. (*Laughing, crosses to the bar and makes another batch of Bloody Marys.*) No. Why don't I get you some ice.

SALLY. (*Looking around quickly—stage whisper.*) No. No, Ellen, what I want is to know why, why knowing me as you do, knowing that I am in a very sensitive, very vulnerable place right now, why, why did you invite me over here on the same day you invited that horrifying woman?

ELLEN. (*Looking to the door.*) She's a wonderful woman and she's going to hear you.

SALLY. She doesn't hear anybody but herself. Who is she?

ELLEN. Do you remember when I had my apartment in New York those two years? She and her son and her husband lived in the apartment next door. They were like my family. Sally, really, try looking beneath the surface.

SALLY. I have and I hate her. Did her son turn out to be a fag? He's got to be a fag.

ELLEN. No.

SALLY. Is he married?

ELLEN. No.

SALLY. How old is he?

ELLEN. I don't know, thirty. Thirty-five.

SALLY. Fag. Is his name David? I find most fags are named David.

ELLEN. Sally, I don't think you realize exactly who her son is. Stuart Risian.

SALLY. (*In utter disbelief* SHE *crosses to* ELLEN *at the bar for her glass of vodka.*) Stuart Risian? Not the famous conductor, Stuart — (*Picks up her glass and crosses back.*) Then he must have been adopted. (*Sits on the sofa.*)

ELLEN. As a matter of fact, he looks exactly like her.

SALLY. (*Sitting on sofa* L.) Probably uses her makeup. She is as horrifying as he is brilliant. They're not close.

ELLEN. It depends on what you mean by "not close."

SALLY. Does he even speak to her?

ELLEN. No.

SALLY. That's what I mean by "not close."

ELLEN. But they will be. They just had a little misunderstanding over a T.V. talk show she was on. It will pass.

SALLY. Oh, God. Oh, my God. (SALLY *starts laughing.*) The mothers of famous people. I saw that show. I saw that —

MAE. (*Not visible yet. Yelling from off stage, interrupting.*) Is it open?

ELLEN. (*Crossing to sliding glass door and opening it.*) Now don't you say a word. Not a word.

(SALLY *tries to stop laughing.* ELLEN *closes the door after* MAE, *then* MAE *gives* SALLY *the purse and sits in chair Downstage* R. *and* SALLY *takes another pill.* ELLEN *crosses to bar for her glass and crosses to chair* L. *to sit.*)

MAE. Ellen, sweetheart, did it ever occur to you to just leave that thing open when company comes. So this place doesn't end up looking like Forest Lawn?

ELLEN. Alright. Alright, Mae, I will leave the doors and windows open if first you tell me you prefer everything inside moist, smoked, rotting or all three.

SALLY. (*A pause.*) Are we ever going to eat? Or just sit around here all day looking like Huey, Louie and Dewey.

ELLEN. I don't know what happened. If Arnold and Florrie aren't here in a few minutes we'll just start. We'll just go ahead and start.

MAE. (*Stands.*) Oh, I hope that's Florrie Cutler you're talking about.

ELLEN. That's right, you know her. So you know she's never late.

SALLY. Who is Florrie Cutler?

ELLEN. She is married to a movie star.

MAE. Brad Cutler.

SALLY. Oh. (SALLY *stands and crosses behind sofa and puts her purse under it and then stands there.*) Oh I've got to practice not looking impressed. I love him.

MAE. Well you can have him. Everyone else has. (MAE *crosses over to sofa and sits* R. *getting cigarettes from purse.*) He's gone to bed with every woman in this country. Except me. And I can't speak for the two of you.

ELLEN. Oh, that's all in the past, not since she and the kids travel everywhere with him now. Today she's coming with the most wonderful man, Arnold Weller, whom I adore.

MAE. Was he ever a press agent?

ELLEN. Right. You know him?

MAE. Oh, sure, he's adorable. (*To* SALLY.) And you'll like Florrie. She's very real. (*Realizes what* SHE *said.*) Then again, maybe you won't.

ELLEN. I asked Florrie to pick Arnold up at his hotel. (MAE *takes out cigarettes and puts one in her mouth and* SALLY *watches . . . then as* MAE *lights her cigarette.*)

SALLY. Oh. Oh. I just hope no one smokes because I'm allergic to smoke.

ELLEN. Sally, we're outdoors.

SALLY. I'm allergic outdoors the same as I am indoors. (MAE, *having held the smoke in her mouth now sneaks it out, puts cigarette out and puts the pack back in her purse.*)

ELLEN. Oh, does that take me back. Sally's only been off cigarettes for what? A year now, isn't it? I've been off over ten years and I never even think about it.

SALLY. (*As* SHE *crosses and sits on sofa* L.) I have a very sensitive constitution. That's why I wear my hair off my face now, if you noticed. I found out that I am allergic to my hair. (SALLY *leans back on sofa causing* MAE, *who has her outstretched arm resting there, to sneakily move her hand away from* SALLY'S *sensitive hair and* SHE *discretely wipes it off.*) Since I notice Ellen gives a resume on all the guests before they arrive I assume she told you about my breakdown.

ELLEN. (*Crossing Up to door.*) Mae arrived here literally one second before you did.

SALLY. Which is probably the only reason she hasn't heard.

ELLEN. (*Laughing.*) I was saving it for when you leave.

MAE. Honey, I would have been on a plane to New York if it wasn't for Ellen's sudden lunch. (*To* ELLEN.) You got anything to tide us over?

ELLEN. Oh Mae, of course. Let me just grab something. (ELLEN *exits to kitchen where we see her opening a jar and getting a dish out and filling it with mints for* MAE. SALLY, *sitting next to* MAE, *puts her hand on* MAE'S *knee and* MAE *looks front, shocked.*)

SALLY. The fact is I was fine until I got on the Garden State Parkway. I came to that first toll booth, and for reasons that to this day I cannot understand I got out of the car and started picking up all that change that people throw that misses those baskets. And I know absolutely the whole thing would never have gotten in the papers if I hadn't taken off all my clothes.

MAE. I imagine it was that more than the change.

SALLY. That drive across the country was the most horrible time in my life. I was arrested in almost every major city. (*Takes out mirror to repair make-up.*)

MAE. People in the midwest do not understand New Yorkers.

ELLEN. (ELLEN *enters and puts down mints on cocktail table.*) Here we go.

SALLY. (*Into mirror.*) Mirror, mirror on the wall, who's the prettiest girl here of all. (*Puts mirror to her ear and laughs. Then.*) Ellen *who*?

ELLEN. (*Laughing.*) Sally. (*Doorbell rings.*) Oh, thank God. They're here. (SHE *crosses Up and opens the sliding glass door.*)

SALLY. (*Aside to* MAE *as* MAE *gets up.*) Here comes her lover. (MAE *hurries to the door as* SALLY *gets up and crosses to the bar.*)

MAE. Oh, Ellen, let me. I cannot wait to see Florrie's face when she sees me.

ELLEN. Go ahead. She'll be thrilled. (MAE *hurries Off through the living room and* ELLEN *slides the door closed, crossing to the bar to mix Bloody Marys.*)

SALLY. (*Caught by* ELLEN *as* SHE *is opening the vodka bottle. Smiles weakly.*) I'm going to put the tiniest bit of vodka in this water glass. (*Tosses the contents of her glass onto the deck causing* ELLEN *to squeal.*)

ELLEN. (*Tries to take the vodka bottle away.*) Sally, you're not. Absolutely no.

SALLY. Yes, I am. If you don't mind. (ELLEN *gives up and wipes the liquid off the floor with a towel from behind the bar as* SALLY *fills her glass.*) You take care of your guests.

(*During the above we see* FLORRIE, *calling "Ellen, Ellen," and* ARNOLD *next to her heading fast for the door with* MAE *behind them shouting "no, no."*

FLORRIE *and* ARNOLD BOTH *rush right into the glass door and go to the floor, with* MAE *rushing up behind them, looking horrified.*

FLORRIE'S *tatting bag came open and* THEY *are picking the yarn, etc., off the floor.* FLORRIE, *laughing all throughout this, is rubbing her forehead and* ARNOLD *is rubbing his knee, lifting it up and down, which makes* FLORRIE *laugh more.*

ELLEN *slides open the glass door and* FLORRIE *and* ARNOLD *enter with* MAE *holding onto* FLORRIE *who is now doubled over laughing.*

FLORRIE *is an aging and pretty girl who is so very ordinary and even common one can't help smile at the incongruity of her and her atmosphere.* SHE *is perpetually smiling or overly serious and compassionate, trying always to help. Her clothes are very attractive and make her enormous Brooklyn accent also incongruous.* SHE *keeps doubling up laughing at what just happened, which explains her.*

ARNOLD *is in his forties. Very elegant, tense and jumpy. His clothes are eastern and casual. Blazer, Khakis, button down shirt, stripped tie, sneakers.* HE *is, to us, likeable because* HE *tries covering his insecurities with a lot of suave . . . and it doesn't always work . . . as* HE *can be easily hurt or made foolish.* HE *rolls up his pant leg examining his in-*

jury. Only we *notice during all this the frequency with which* SALLY *drinks.*

ELLEN *slides open the glass door and* EVERYONE *is talking all at once and in a rush as* THEY *enter.*)

ELLEN. I don't believe this. Who could believe this?

MAE. I opened the front door and they didn't even stop!

ARNOLD. (*Limping to chair Down* R. *crossing in front of sofa.*) Why did you close that door?

ELLEN. I didn't close the door. I just didn't open it yet. (FLORRIE, *still Up at the door, laughs.*)

ARNOLD. The miracle is that we're alive. That we are not just impressed forever on that glass. (*To* FLORRIE.) What is funny?

FLORRIE. (*Laughing, to* ELLEN.) Did you see what I did when I fell? I grabbed at my skirt so nobody could see up my dress. Like who's gonna look?

ARNOLD. I looked. And I cannot remember anything ever exciting me more.

MAE. (*Crossing Down* L., *putting* FLORRIE's *knitting bag on the chair* L. *then crosses next to the bar.*) Ellen, you really should let everybody know the kind of glass cleaner you use. It's remarkable.

ELLEN. (*Crosses Downstage in front of sofa to* AR-NOLD.) Is everybody *well* is all I want to know.

ARNOLD. (*Puts leg up on coffee table.*) How swollen is it? It's swollen, isn't it?

SALLY. (*Behind bar still. To* MAE *standing next to the bar.*) That man is not her lover.

ELLEN. It's not swollen, Arnold. Walk on it though. And they say the worst thing you can do for a bad leg is complain. (ARNOLD *crosses to chair Downstage* R., *wipes it off with a hankie, and sits wiping off his pants, jacket and exploring his knee.*)

FLORRIE. I haven't had a good laugh since I left New York. I haven't had a good anything since I left New York. I say when the world comes to an end California will still have one year to go. (SHE *screams.*) Mae! Mae Risian! I just saw that's you! (SHE *crosses* L. *and hugs* MAE.)

MAE. Who the hell do you think let you in?

FLORRIE. I thought at the door you were the maid. Imagine actually seeing someone you know at Ellen's house.

(ELLEN *takes* FLORRIE'S *wrap and* ARNOLD'S *briefcase and exits through the living room and Off* L.)

MAE. Ellen's just one of those people who likes to keep her friends separate. It's her nature. And I know this one too. (*Indicating* ARNOLD.)

ARNOLD. (*He gets up.*) Oh, what terrible thing did I do? Was it something disgusting? Should I be ashamed?

MAE. You represented my son Stuart a way, way back. Years ago.

ARNOLD. Oh, my God, Stuart Risian. Look. I'm sweating all over. Don't do that to people.

MAE. By the way, you got very good legs.

ARNOLD. I'm married. (*He sits chair* R.)

(*As* FLORRIE *organizes her knitting and sits on sofa* L., MAE *crosses and sits in chair* L.)

FLORRIE. Mae, you been on my mind. I swear. This is so peculiar. Try not to look too close. I had one day's notice to get five kids stashed somewhere and rush out here for Ellen's emergency lunch. (ELLEN *enters and stands behind sofa.*) So, Ellen, I'm so impressed you wrote a book.

ELLEN. Yes, I did.

ARNOLD. And?

ELLEN. And what?

ARNOLD. Is it a touchy subject?

ELLEN. No, it is not a touchy subject.

FLORRIE. Ellen, tell us about the book.

ELLEN. I will, I will. My plan is to get you drunk, and feed you a lot and then send you each home with a copy.

SALLY. (*As* SHE *passes behind* ELLEN, *going Upstage near the fence.*) She won't talk about the book.

ELLEN. No, no, no, I just don't want to talk about it yet. First Florrie, I want to talk about you. Is your husband's movie finished yet?

FLORRIE. Oh, God no. And now there's another one after this. Don't ask. Mae, you hate it here? Someone must have tipped this country on its end and everything that wasn't screwed down fell into California.

ELLEN. (*Sits on right arm of couch.*) Oh, Arnold, I forgot to ask how the new play is going. Arnold's wife is maybe the best playwright in the world.

ARNOLD. Betty Pearlman.

ELLEN. Certainly the most famous. How's it going?

ARNOLD. (*Smiles, put his forefinger and thumb together then says.*) Disaster.

ELLEN. Oh, Betty is so lucky to have you around. (ELLEN *crosses to bar and wipes up floor where water was spilled.*)

ARNOLD. *How* am I around? I should be at the matinee right *now*. She forced me out here. She did. (*Holding knee lifts his leg up and down.*) You don't have an X-ray machine around here, do you?

ELLEN. (*Holding up container of Bloody Marys.*) Better. I know I forced each of you out here today and I'll explain why right after we eat.

FLORRIE. (*To* SALLY *who just sat down next to her on sofa* R.) Hi. I'm Florrie Cutler. Nice to meet you.

SALLY. I'm little, insignificant Sally Stern.

ELLEN. (*Crosses to them.*) Oh, Sally, I'm sorry. This is Arnold Weller, too. I'm just not in charge today. (*She closes the sliding glass door.*)

ARNOLD. You're not closing that door are you?

ELLEN. Arnold, everyone has learned where it is and how it works so it cannot possibly be a problem. (*Moves back to bar.*)

FLORRIE. Ellen, if you don't mind a suggestion? You put those little decals on the door. Little fishes and mermaids and things.

SALLY. A skull and crossbones would be more appropriate.

FLORRIE. (*Sniffing.*) Is that smoke?

ARNOLD. (*Looking around.*) I can even taste it.

ELLEN. (*Hurriedly. Getting them off the subject.*) Don't worry. When the smoke gets too thick an oxygen mask will drop down.

ARNOLD. Ellen, I'm desperate to hear about your book.

ELLEN. And I'm desperate to tell you. How was your drive out here? Other than long.

FLORRIE. (*Indicating* ARNOLD.) Your wiseacre friend there beat me ten dollars at backgammon.

ELLEN. Oh, isn't that a sensible thing to do when you're driving.

FLORRIE. No. We dropped my husband the movie star off at the studio so we got my husband the movie star's chauffeur who's going to pick us up too . . . if he can. You should see up your—

MAE. (*Interrupting.*) Don't you ever stick around the studio and just watch?

FLORRIE. No. Oh, Mae, you want a happy life? Never go anyplace where you don't have credentials. (*To the* OTHERS.) Oh, see, Mae. See. See, Mae can't connect me with chauffeurs. She connects me with my old beauty shop where I was a hairdresser twelve years. (*Turning to* SALLY *and holding out a strand of her own hair.*) What happened, you wonder. (*Takes out her tatting and begins working.*)

ARNOLD. (*Looking around.*) Ellen? May I use your phone? Or do they have them this far out?

ELLEN. Of course, Arnold. (ARNOLD *crosses* L. *as* ELLEN *takes phone from under bar and puts it on Down* L. *table.*) Right here. Or if you want to be private—

ARNOLD. (*At the small table next to the bar, sitting on the table with the phone and dialing.*) No, no, no. Doesn't that ocean sound drive you crazy? I could never sleep to that. I'd have to pretend it was the traffic.

ELLEN. Listen, I understand that in New York they sell these little machines that *make* the sound of the ocean to put you to sleep.

ARNOLD. Ah, but that's the Atlantic.

ELLEN. (*To* FLORRIE *and* ARNOLD.) Would you both like a quick drink before I serve my fantastic surprise lunch?

SALLY. Nothing for me.

ARNOLD. I'd love one.

FLORRIE. Why not?

MAE. Me too.

(ELLEN *bringing them drinks, taking empty glass from* MAE *back to bar and filling it.*)

FLORRIE. Your friend and I would have been here on time. But halfway up the coast you should see. There's nothing but cars backed up as far as you can look. The enormous mountain right down your street is moving, the policeman said, right across the highway.

ELLEN. (*Bringing the drink to* MAE.) Oh, is that happening again? (ELLEN *goes Up to the large dining table Upstage* L. *and puts a table cloth and napkins on it.*)

FLORRIE. Again? The mountain is collapsing and she says, "oh, is that happening again." Ellen, it's moved more than halfway across the highway. Like it's going to Mohammed. They had to back up all the cars and turn them around and we had to go back and around these terrifying hairpin turns and then so high up I couldn't look out the window then down like this. I was so glad your friend there plays backgammon.

SALLY. (SHE *has jumped up, very upset, as* SHE *crosses to* ELLEN *at table.*) Ellen, how are we supposed to get home? I would hate to be stuck in this godforsaken place.

ELLEN. I'd hate to *have* you stuck in this godforsaken place. (ELLEN *crosses to the bar getting silverware and crosses back to dining table folding silverware in napkins.*) Don't worry. They usually clear it in no time at all.

SALLY. I think I'm going to have a touch more tonic. (*Goes to the bar and fills her glass with vodka again with a glare from* ELLEN *then crosses to far Downstage* R. *looking Off at beach.*)

ARNOLD. Can you believe that there is no one at the switchboard at the Beverly Hills Hotel? My God, it's like being in Singapore or someplace.

ELLEN. We go at a slower pace in California.

ARNOLD. (*Turning to the* OTHERS.) Is there an understatement of the year award? (*To* ELLEN.) Oh, I forgot, we saw John in the hotel last night.

ELLEN. (*Very nervous.*) Oh? Did you speak to him?

ARNOLD. No.

ELLEN. Good.

ARNOLD. Why is that "good"?

ELLEN. I meant "good" that you saw him. I'll tell him.

ARNOLD. Where is he today?

ELLEN. Who?

ARNOLD. John.

ELLEN. Working.

MAE. At the Beverly Hills Hotel?

ELLEN. More for anyone.

SALLY. (*As* ARNOLD *lights a cigarette.*) Oh, is he going to smoke?

ARNOLD. Yes, he is. It conditions his lungs for the smog.

MAE. (*Crossing to* ARNOLD.) Give me a drag.

ARNOLD. (*He gives it to her and* SHE *takes a puff.*) What is this, the boys' room? (MAE *takes quick puffs.*) (*To* ELLEN.) Anyway, he was getting on a elevator. (*Takes cigarette away from* MAE *who is puffing fast.*) It's just a cigarette. (SHE *crosses and sits in chair* L. *and exhaling smoke.*) (*To* ELLEN.) What was he doing there? (*Into phone.*) Hell . . . Hello? Is this the Beverly Hills Hotel?

(ELLEN *opens the sliding glass door and goes into the kitchen and we see her Offstage through the kitchen window getting things ready for the luncheon.*)

ARNOLD. (*Continued.*) Oh, I was certain I had dialed an incorrect number because you took so long to answer. (*Pause.*) Yes, well everyone in this world is busy. That's the reason some hotels maintain staffs.

What? (*Turns to the* GROUP. *Astonished.*)
Unbelievable. She just told me to "hold on."

(FLORRIE *continues tatting and* MAE *has opened her collar and tries to get some sun.*)

FLORRIE. Do they have that terrible radio music playing?

ARNOLD. No.

FLORRIE. Then don't complain. So, Mae, what the hell's going on around here? She drags me out here because she's finished this book so I get out here and she doesn't say word one about the book.

ARNOLD. I'm married to a writer. That means something is up. (*Pointing to* FLORRIE'S *knitting.*) Look. Look how she can do that.

FLORRIE. What? Oh, what's to look. I do it to keep busy. I can't stand quiet and I can't stand nothing to do. I'm from New York, I take this to the bathroom. So, Mae, what's the big secret?

MAE. I have nothing to say.

ARNOLD. Maybe the books stinks. (ELLEN *slides open kitchen window and puts platters of food on the counter in front of it.*) (*Into phone again.*) No, I was not talking to you. No, I doubt that there is any reason to be connected to the message desk judging by the way you run your switchboard. All I want is for someone there to instruct the maid that my wife left a note for her this morning—Oh, this is Betty Pearlman's husband, Mr. Weller, in room 203, and my wife left a note this morning to the maid on exactly how we want the bed to be made. We cannot sleep unless the sheets are done in a certain, very specific way. Did the maid—I say did the maid—please let me finish. Did the maid see the note?

Well, then who does know? Yes, please tell the floor maid to look for it because neither of us speaks Spanish. And there is a large diagram with the note. Now if my wife calls I am at 456-6921. And would you have the maid save the diagram please, we travel with it. Thank you. (*He hangs up.*)

ELLEN. (*Enters with salad bowl.*) Everything's finally coming and it's wonderful. Nobody look, Arnold. (ELLEN *moves three large platters from kitchen window ledge to the Up* L. *table as* ARNOLD *watches.*)

ARNOLD. (*Still carrying his lighted cigarette.*) I just got a glimpse. And I'm speechless. (*He takes a drag and crosses Down* R.)

SALLY. You will be when they remove your voice-box.

(ARNOLD *is passing her and now blows his exhaled smoke right in her face, then continues on and sits on the sofa* R. *next to* FLORRIE. *After an annoyed moment* SALLY *sits in the chair Downstage* R.)

ELLEN. (ELLEN *makes salad dressing.*) Oh, I must say I am very impressed with myself.

FLORRIE. Let me help.

ELLEN. No. Nobody help. Nobody even look.

MAE. (*Looking at ocean.*) I'm going to be real glad to be home tomorrow.

ELLEN. (*Pours dressing on salad.*) Oh, but Mae, I thought you liked it here.

MAE. Oh, I do.

ELLEN. You like the weather.

MAE. Crazy about the weather.

ELLEN. You like the people.

MAE. Love the people.

ELLEN. You have friends here.

MAE. I know.

ELLEN. Then why are you going back?

MAE. The ocean's on the wrong side.

ARNOLD. You've missed your calling. You should be on T.V. (HE *puts out his cigarette.*)

SALLY. Oh, she has been on T.V. (MAE *looks up, stunned.*)

ELLEN. (*Stops tossing salad a moment.*) Sally.

MAE. (*Looks around. Then.*) Did everybody here see that show?

FLORRIE. I don't want to discuss it, Mae, but don't ever do another one.

MAE. Is there one person in the world who did not see that television show? I don't even know what I said that night because I was so nervous that that host was going to ask me is my son a homosexual.

SALLY. Why?

MAE. Because everybody thinks "musician," "not married," "over thirty," "homosexual." And he's not.

SALLY. How do you know he's not?

MAE. Because I asked him.

ARNOLD. Maybe he just said "no" not to disappoint you.

MAE. Listen, when I asked him actually in some way I was counting on that he *was* and I was all prepared to be real understanding and say things like, "It's not *who* you love it's *that* you love." (*Slight pause.*) And crap like that.

ELLEN. But the announcer never even asked.

MAE. I know. He didn't ask and didn't ask. So finally at the end I just blurted out, "And for anyone's information, he is not a homosexual."

ELLEN. I nearly died.

FLORRIE. I wet my pants.

MAE. But that show is the whole reason I came out here for a few months. So everybody would forget it. That's not the exact truth. I mean, it's not all my son. You see, living next door to me in New York is the sweetest, most wonderful, good man I have ever known. And (*Crosses to* ELLEN.) I have always had very good luck with the people who live next door to me.

ELLEN. (*They hug.*) Oh, Mae.

MAE. Anyway, a couple of months after my husband's funeral he up and asked me to marry him. I couldn't get over it.

ELLEN. What's his name?

MAE. Mort. It'd be Mort and Mae.

ARNOLD. Sounds like a comedy team.

FLORRIE. Is he Jewish?

MAE. He's a Christian Scientist.

FLORRIE. Oh, then he *was* Jewish.

MAE. Anyway, I had to say no. It's much too soon. I'll tell you frankly I really thought about marrying that Christian Scientist. Hell, I even cleared out my medicine cabinet.

ELLEN. (*Laughing.*) Oh, Mae, Mae, sometimes I know exactly what John meant when he said you were unmistakable in my book. (THEY ALL *stop and look at* MAE *as* ELLEN *tries to cover her blunder and tosses salad again.*)

MAE. (*Puzzled.*) Should I go out and come in again?

ELLEN. (*Still working at the table behind them, salting, tasting food.*) Well, you know when you write, you base things on specific people.

MAE. (*Interrupting.*) Hold the phone, Ellen. Hold the phone. Am I in this new book?

ELLEN. No. Of course not. I mean not actually. No more than Arnold or Florrie or Sally.

SALLY. Me?

ARNOLD. I beg your pardon.

FLORRIE. Did she say "Florrie"?

ELLEN. I mean, the book is fiction. But naturally I used my friends to base my characters on.

MAE. (*Crosses Up to* ELLEN.) Well you told me *they* were in it, but you never told me *I* was in it.

ELLEN. Well, I never told you you weren't in it.

SALLY. (*Gets up and crosses to the bar.*) Oh, my God! I just hope I'm going deaf.

ARNOLD. (*Crosses toward Downstage* C.) Screw this lunch. Where's that book?

FLORRIE. How do you know when you're having a heart attack?

SALLY. What did you *say* about me?

ELLEN. Now come on, come on. I'm sorry I slipped and brought it up.

FLORRIE. Why in hell would anybody put me in a book?

ARNOLD. Did you force us out here to warn us that someone we used to like very much had suddenly turned on us?

ELLEN. Well, I certainly didn't want you to wander into a bookstore and discover it there.

ARNOLD. What does that mean? What does that mean what you just said?

MAE. Be still my heart.

FLORRIE. Discover *what* in a bookstore? Discover what?

SALLY. I can't stand it.

TOGETHER
(THEY *all come to her.*)

ELLEN. I didn't mean that. Let's please drop it.

ARNOLD. Let's please not.

MAE. Could I have my copy now?

ELLEN. Oh, Mae, when you finish it you'll be —

ARNOLD. (*Interrupting.*) You'll be found dead on the floor.

ELLEN. Please for now *eat*. Let's not even think about it.

FLORRIE. That's like telling you not to think of an elephant.

ARNOLD. Could we read it first and eat this condemned man's hearty meal later?

ELLEN. Oh, wait a minute. Wait a minute. Is there anyone here who honestly, really doesn't trust me and wants to read it now? (*Then very quickly before anyone responds.*) Good. Then it's settled. (ELLEN *moves behind the table waiting to serve them.*)

MAE. Settled?
FLORRIE. I don't think so.
ARNOLD. Excuse me? } TOGETHER
SALLY. I'm panicky.

ELLEN. Everybody, everybody now sit any place you want. We're just beachy-beachy today. (*Then pointing specifically to Stage* R. *chair.*) Arnold, you can sit over there. (*To couch* R.) Mae, you over here. (*To sofa* L.) Florrie, over there (*To Down* L. *chair.*) and Sally, here. (FLORRIE *has sat in the chair Down* L. *and* SALLY *crosses to* FLORRIE.)

SALLY. Get up. (FLORRIE *goes to her designated spot, moving* MAE. MAE *moves* ARNOLD *and as* HE *goes to Down* R. *chair* HE *says.*)

ARNOLD. (*To* ELLEN.) I thought we could sit anywhere we wanted. Beachy-beachy.

ELLEN. Oh, you can. Sit there, Arnold. (*Uncovering the food as* ARNOLD *sits.*) Now. This is a special treat. You've all been away from your New York so long I thought I would remedy that. (*Crosses between couch and chair.*)

ARNOLD. First may I ask one question about this book?

ELLEN. No. So . . . I had all of this flown in from New York. (*Crosses back to table Up* L.)

FLORRIE. She had it flown in. Can you imagine what must be in that book?

ELLEN. I went down to the airport and I picked it up this morning.

FLORRIE. I would like to know who in the hell here can eat it?

ELLEN. Everyone here can eat it. And everyone better eat it. Did you see the Goldberg's pizza. (*Crosses to them with pizza and back to table again.*) I wanted it all to be really a treat.

FLORRIE. "Treat" is not the word. "Bribe" is the word.

ARNOLD. Will you at least tell us the title?

ELLEN. No, Arnold, we're eating.

ARNOLD. What, is the title repellent?

ELLEN. (*Crosses to them with tray showing it, then back to table.*) Mae, that cornbeef is from the Carnegie delicatessen. The sturgeon is from Barney Greengrass. (MAE *rises and crosses to* ELLEN *who fixes her a plate.*)

ARNOLD. Who cares? What I care about is why you never mentioned all of this until this book is practically out?

FLORRIE. Why do you think? Because we'll be so happy?

ELLEN. This is all so stupid because I know you're going to love it.

SALLY. (*Gets up, crosses behind bar.*) Oh, my God. I'm in an expose.

MAE. Now let's all just eat, since she's positive we're going to love it. (MAE *crosses back to couch* R. *with plate and sits.*)

ELLEN. And, oh Mae, that Nova Scotia is from Murray's.

ARNOLD. (*Crosses to* ELLEN *at table.*) I don't care about Murray's. What I care about is what is the worst thing I do in your book?

ELLEN. Ask questions. And everything else is from Zabars.

ARNOLD. May I ask one small question about the book?

ELLEN. No.

ARNOLD. (*Crosses to* FLORRIE *on sofa* L.) Would you please ask her if this is one of those "tell-all" books.

FLORRIE. (*Getting up, crossing to* ELLEN, *speaking directly to her.*) Those books are sickening.

ARNOLD. Have you read any of them?

FLORRIE. (*Turns head to* ARNOLD.) Every one. (*Looks back at* ELLEN.)

SALLY. (*Still behind bar.*) Arnold, how funny you're this worried. I mean to look at you there seems so little to tell. (ARNOLD *turns to the rest, shocked.*) Oh, now I didn't mean that cruelly.

ARNOLD. Oh, did you mean it kindly?

MAE. Ellen, speaking of cruelly, tell me you didn't put anything in this book about that television show.

ELLEN. (ELLEN *crosses between couch and chair* L.) First of all, if the book is about anyone, it's about me.

ARNOLD. Wait a minute.

ELLEN. No, Arnold, now I'm not responding to one more question. (ELLEN *crosses back and puts salad on five salad dishes.*)

ARNOLD. (*Crosses to* MAE, *stands at sofa* L.) Wait a minute. Did I see that show?

MAE. God, Ellen. With your book and that television show I would have got less attention taking off all my clothes on the Garden State Parkway.

SALLY. How dare you mock me.

MAE. I only meant we all have our problems.

SALLY. I was insane last year.

MAE. Well, thank God you're well now. (*Puts down food.*) Now I can't eat. Well, I'll eat. I just won't enjoy it. (*Picks up food and eats.*)

ELLEN. Why is no one else eating? This perfect luncheon and no one else is eating.

FLORRIE. (*Pacing behind sofa.*) Because our stomachs are in knots.

ARNOLD. (*Leaning into* MAE, *remembering.*) It was all those mothers of those famous people. I just didn't see the end.

FLORRIE. (*To* ELLEN *as* SHE *continues pacing.*) You cannot tell people they're in your book and then expect them to eat a fun lunch.

} TOGETHER

SALLY. (*To* MAE.) I wasn't going to say anything but I saw that mother show.

MAE. And I wasn't going to say anything but *I* read about your striptease.

FLORRIE. What striptease?

SALLY. I am not here to discuss my private life in front of strangers.

ELLEN. (*To* ALL.) Sally's going through a divorce.

SALLY. (*Shouting, steps out from behind bar.*) I am not going through a divorce.

ELLEN. (*Crosses down below dining room table.*) I don't know why I keep saying "divorce."

SALLY. Do you have me taking off my clothes in your smarmy book?

ELLEN. No I don't. (*Crosses Up behind dining table again.*)

ARNOLD. If I could only remember what I told her.

} TOGETHER

ELLEN. And why do you all assume that my book is

mean and terrrible?

FLORRIE. Because we've all been playing with the big kids for a long time now.

SALLY. (*Shouting.*) Oh, my God. It was an emotional upheaval. Don't you understand? It was an emotional upheaval!

ARNOLD. (*To* MAE.) I think she's having one right now.

MAE. Don't tell me, tell Congressman Stern.

FLORRIE. (*Crosses toward* SALLY, *ends Up* L. *of sofa.*) Oh, I worship George Stern.

ARNOLD. (*Crossing Downstage* C.) Was he your husband?

SALLY. *Is* my husband. He *is* my husband. Despite what Ellen may have told you secretly before you got here.

ELLEN. (*Crosses around table Down to* SALLY.) I don't talk about my friends.

FLORRIE. (*To* ARNOLD.) She just writes about them.

ARNOLD. Do you realize every person here is related to somebody very, very famous? My wife, your son, your husband . . . (*To* SALLY.) What was your reaction to the announcement they were expecting the baby?

ELLEN. (*Laughing, getting books from behind bar and passing them out, keeping it light.*) Uh, oh, actually I was planning to hand these out when you were all on your way home. But why? Why wait? We can read and eat. Here. Here it is. The book. It comes out in a week, so you have the very first copies. Now the publisher has this whole silly paranoia about lawsuits so he's ordered me to get each one of you to sign these silly waivers. Or he won't bring the book out at all. I tried to explain to him that everyone's a composite but you know—

(ELLEN *energetically hands out books but when* SHE *reaches* SALLY *with the book and* SALLY *stands so still, taking the book but staring still at* ARNOLD, ELLEN *is stopped.* ELLEN *is pained at how to handle this gently.*)

SALLY. (SALLY *crosses and sits on* L. *arm of chair* L.) When was that?

ARNOLD. This morning the story was all over the news that they were expecting a baby and this afternoon he confirmed it. Do you mean I am telling you this for the first time?

MAE. I think you're telling all of us for the first time.

FLORRIE. (*To* SALLY, *with compassion.*) Well . . . he's dead in politics.

ARNOLD. Oh, please, please. In New York that'll get him another hundred thousand votes. (THEY ALL *look at him and* HE *turns and lights a cigarette.*)

ELLEN. (*To* SALLY, *straight but sympathetic.*) Oh, Sally, I knew when you got here today, you didn't know. I should have told you. I'm sorry.

SALLY. She got him. She got him with the oldest trick in the world. (*To* ARNOLD.) Give me one of those cigarettes. (*As* ARNOLD *offers her his package* SHE *instead takes his lighted cigarette.*)

MAE. Me too.

FLORRIE. Oh what the hell. (*Reaches for a cigarette.*)

ELLEN. (*Reaching.*) I want one too. (*A stunned* ARNOLD *gives, then lights* MAE's *and* FLORRIE's *and* ELLEN's *cigarettes. Now there is a distant helicopter sound increasing.*)

SALLY. Having had nothing but tonic water all afternoon, I don't think anybody would begrudge me a drink. (SHE *lifts vodka bottle to her lips and swigs.*)

ELLEN. Sally—

SALLY. (*Turning, mocking, angry, challenging.*) Ellen.

PILOT. (*VO.*) (*Voice coming from the speaker system*

of the helicopter.) Attention. Attention. All residents of Malibu. (THEY ALL *look up at the helicopter except* SAL- LY *who stays at the bar drinking.*) A brush fire is extend- ing into the hills of the Malibu residential area. Repeat. A brush fire is extending into the hills of the Malibu residential area. All movement in this area is henceforth restricted. Please obey the directions of the firemen patroling the beach areas. Remain in your homes, but stand by for possible evacuation. Do not panic and remain in your homes, but stand by for possi- ble evacuation. (*The fading last lines indicate the helicopter is moving into the distance and ultimately disappears though the* PEOPLE *speak the following over the VO.*)

ELLEN. Don't worry. It's in the hills.

FLORRIE. Ellen, the hills are right across the street.

ELLEN. Nothing's going to happen. (*To* ARNOLD.) Nothing's going to happen.

ARNOLD. It's already happening.

ELLEN. No one panic. This always happens.

FLORRIE. This always happens? (SALLY *walks from the bar toward exit Down* R. *swigging from the vodka bottle.*)

ELLEN. Try and stay outdoors till it's over.

MAE. I don't need to try. Nothing would get me in there.

ELLEN. Sally, where are you going?

SALLY. (*Without turning back.*) I'm going to take a little walk on the beach. (SHE *exits Downstage* R.)

ELLEN. (*Following her, calling.*) Oh, Sally, should you? Why don't you hold off? (*Turns to the* OTHERS.) I don't know what to do for her. Should I go with her?

FLORRIE. We'll watch her. What can happen on the beach?

MAE. Oh, poor soul. Let her go.

ARNOLD. (*Pacing.*) Oh, she makes me so crazy. Wouldn't *you* want to know? If it were I, I'd certainly want to know.

ELLEN. (*Crossing to the table.*) Oh, Arnold, if Betty left you you wouldn't even be able to walk on the beach.

FLORRIE. (*Putting cigarette out on* MAE'S *plate.*) Please, I never pick up a newspaper I don't expect to read that exact Spanish news about *my* husband. You think I go with him everywhere because it's so much fun? Grow up. (*Sits on sofa* R.)

MAE. (*Standing between couch and chair* R.) Arnold, I don't know you real well, but you just did a real bad thing.

ARNOLD. (*Sits on small Down* R. *chair pulling off shoes, socks, and rolling up pants quickly.*) What is this "real well," "real bad," "real" everything? Whatever happened to the word, "very." I don't know why I said it. It's this whole terrible thing we're going through with the show and now this book. I'll go try to explain. I'll just go and try to explain. (*Fully dressed in jacket and tie, pants rolled up.* HE *starts exiting to the beach and* HE *is stopped, aghast. Covering his face.*) Oh my God. Oh, my God. (THEY *run toward him yelling "what" "what's wrong" etc.*) Two firemen are dragging her from the ocean. (FLORRIE *and* MAE *scream and chatter and kick off their shoes as* THEY ALL *prepare to run down there.* ARNOLD *paces and moans.*) Oh my God, oh my God, oh my God, what have I done?

ELLEN. I'll get her. Arnold, you stay here. Mae, Florrie, you come too. (ELLEN *gets beach towel from chest, brings it to* ARNOLD. MAE *takes off suitcoat and rolls up sleeves.*)

FLORRIE. You come with me, Mae, you're good at

this. (SHE *exits.*)

ELLEN. Arnold, fix someplace for her to lie down. (ELLEN *exits.*)

ARNOLD. Oh, my God. What have I done?

MAE. (*Slapping his cheeks.*) Arnold, Arnold. Fix someplace for her to lie down and shut up. And have something to drink that will warm her. (*Takes off shoes, exiting.*) And I don't mean brandy.

(MAE *exits. Distant Offstage* VOICES *are heard throughout the following and the helicopter VO is repeated again. Then later on during this, the helicopter message is repeated a third time, but far away while* ARNOLD *fusses and talks to himself.* HE *immediately clears everything off of the coffee table and joins it to the chair so together they make a bed.* HE *moves the little phone table Downstage* L. *Upstage of this makeshift bed.* HE *stops a second, then turns the phone around so it can be used. Next* HE *goes to the bar and runs back with an aspirin bottle and a box of tissues which* HE *puts down on the phone table too. Even stopping to raise and fluff up the top tissue.* HE *runs back to the bar, grabs the wine bottle and a glass and places them next to the box of tissues. Then* HE *takes the beach towel* ELLEN *just gave him and uses it as a sheet over the makeshift bed, tucking in the bottom and even pulling one corner back for accessibility. Next* HE *spots the flower pot next to the bar and pulls off a flower . . . looks around for a container and puts the flower in his mouth as* HE *opens a small bottle of Perrier and sticks the flower in the bottle and places it on the small table above the makeshift bed. Then, finished,* HE *turns and hurries Upstage, remembering at the very last second not to run into the sliding glass door,* HE *opens it and gets the cof-fee pot and cup out of the kitchen. During this the* WOMEN'S *Offstage* VOICES *approach and* HE *stands nervously above his makeshift hospital.*)

ELLEN. (*Offstage.*) That's fine. We got her. (*The* THREE *of them are heard offstage.*)

MAE. (*Offstage.*) That's Congressman Stern's wife, so all of Washington is going to be real grateful.

FLORRIE. (*Offstage.*) Thank you very much. Very much.

ELLEN. (*Offstage.*) We'll take her from here. We're so grateful. (THEY *appear.* ALL THREE *now wet carrying* SALLY, *cross the stage.*)

ARNOLD. (*Rushing from the kitchen with the coffee pot and cup, pouring, as* HE *hurries to the makeshift bed to put the cup down.*) Is she alright? How is she?

MAE. She's fine. She just threw up.

(*Hurrying straight across Stage, seemingly headed for* ARNOLD'S *makeshift bed,* THEY *suddenly turn and veer Upstage, out the glass door and exit up the steps* L. ARNOLD *is stunned.*)

SALLY. I'm going to throw up again. (THEY *drop her and* SALLY *rushes upstairs with* MAE *and* FLORRIE *after her.* ALL *talking at once.*)

ELLEN. (*Entering the deck, to* ARNOLD *who is now standing in the doorway.*) Arnold, is that coffee hot?

ARNOLD. Yes.

ELLEN. Take it up to her. (HE *exits thru glass door up the stairs. Seeing books,* SHE *gathers them up and puts them behind the bar.*) (*To herself.*) This is definitely not the time. (*Calls upstairs.*) Mae, Florrie. Come down and take off those wet clothes. I'll bring you some robes.

(ELLEN *exits Up* R. *gate to yard area to get the robes.*

Sound of the helicopter approaching again as an even more wet MAE *and* FLORRIE *come hurrying down the stairs rushing to get out of their clothes. Out on the deck* MAE *is down to her slip and* FLORRIE *to her camisole when simultaneously* THEY *stop as the* PILOT *flies over speaking and* THEY *stare up at him as* THEY *realize* THEY'RE *being watched and try subtly to cover themselves as* THEY *listen in embarrassment.*)

PILOT. (*VO.*) Attention. Attention all residents of Malibu. Water pressure alert, phase one, is now in effect. Firemen on the beach will be checking water supply and pressure. Use no water until further notice. Repeat. Use no water until further notice.

(*During the above,* ELLEN *enters with the robes, gives* FLORRIE *one then goes up and closes the glass door. Then crosses Down to* MAE *and helps her into the other robe as we hear helicopters in distance repeating the announcement.*)

MAE. (*Getting into robe.*) Ellen, if that guy in the helicopter asks for our phone number, give it to him.

(ELLEN *is taking* ARNOLD'S *makeshift bed apart and putting cushions back on sofa.*)

ELLEN. I don't think she needs a doctor. Does anybody else? (*Takes towel off of chairs, sits on sofa* R. *and dries herself.*)
FLORRIE. (*Sits on arm of sofa* L. *shaking out her*

hair.) Ask me she needs a whole hospital. Did you see all the reporters covering the fire?

ELLEN. I sure did. Thanks to our friend here now it could get into the papers.

MAE. (*Sits in chair Down* R.) I thought they'd be more careful if she *was* somebody.

ELLEN. I feel so sorry for her.

MAE. Ellen, with the mountain and the fire and all how will John ever get back?

ELLEN. (*A pause.*) John's not coming back, Mae. John moved out. I'm sure you figured that out.

FLORRIE. (*Touching* ELLEN's *shoulder.*) When? When did that happen?

ELLEN. It just happened.

MAE. Over what?

ELLEN. He just misunderstood. He said he felt hurt and shocked — devastated.

MAE. (*Takes* ELLEN's *hand.*) Well, sweetheart, count on us to help.

ELLEN. You can't help. He just *read* it wrong.

(FLORRIE *removes her hand and* MAE *removes her hand and* THEY *sit back stunned.*)

FLORRIE. What, your book? He walked out over your book?

ELLEN. And he's the one who insisted he wouldn't read it until it came out.

MAE. What did you do to John in your book?

ELLEN. I didn't do anything to John in the book and I just hope and pray he's off understanding that.

FLORRIE. (*Looking around.*) Ellen? Where did you put the books?

ELLEN. I just don't think . . . I just don't think this is

the atmosphere for it.

FLORRIE. This atmosphere is just fine. Fine. Oh yeah, there. (*Goes behind bar and gets out two books.*) Since everybody today is writing these assassination books about their so-called friends and families . . . to the point some of them even move out . . . we will all feel better, I'm sure, after we read the book. (*Hands* MAE *a book then sits on the* L. *arm of the sofa getting right into the book.* MAE *puts on her glasses.*)

ELLEN. Do you honestly think now is the time?

FLORRIE. Yes. In fact it's past time.

MAE. It's the perfect time.

ELLEN. (*Getting up, crossing to bar.*) Fine. Read it. I wanted to explain some things, a few things to you, but fine. I'm sure you'll enjoy it very much.

ARNOLD. (*Appearing on the upper balcony still carrying the coffee pot.*) She's either asleep or she just passed out. What are you doing?

ELLEN. (*Looking up.*) They're reading my book. (*Pours a drink.*)

ARNOLD. (*Teasing it.*) Did you get to me yet? (*Turns to exit.*)

FLORRIE. The first line. She gets to all of us.

ARNOLD. (*Turns back.*) What's the first line?

FLORRIE. (*Reads.*) "My mother always told me to stick with the winners but if I had I never would have met my four friends." (THEY *turn and look at* ELLEN *who downs the drink as.*)

CURTAIN

END ACT ONE

ACT TWO

PLACE: *The same.*

TIME: *Later the same day. As this scene continues we go into dusk and ultimately to night.*

The curtain rises and FLORRIE, *in her robe and hair in curlers, is alone on the deck seated on the sofa reading intensely.* MAE, *also in a robe and curlers, can be seen through the kitchen window, seated inside at the counter wearing small reading glasses, and also reading intensely.* ARNOLD, *now with his jacket off, tie undone, is visible in the living room in a chair and also reading intensely. A second.* ALL THREE *turn a page simultaneously.*

FLORRIE, *dropping her jaw, lets her hand go to her mouth and* SHE *lets out a tiny sound of shock and* SHE *tears off a piece of paper and puts it in the book marking the page (There are many markers sticking out.)*

A second later MAE *in the kitchen suddenly puts her hand over her mouth to stifle a laugh.*

ARNOLD, *with a gasp, points to his place in the book as* HE *gets up and hurries to the living room door, and as* HE *opens his mouth to speak to* FLORRIE, MAE *begins laughing and laughing almost uncontrollably until* SHE *looks up and sees the* OTHER TWO *just staring at her.*

SHE *tries, but* MAE *cannot stop her laughing and exits the kitchen and up the steps with her laughter totally out of control as* SHE *disappears. Then* ARNOLD *turns and crosses to his chair in the living room where* HE *resumes reading.*

The doorbell rings three times. ARNOLD *shields his face
with his hand and* FLORRIE *looks to where* SHE *can
hide but instead just turns her back on the room
and continues reading.* ELLEN *enters in a new outfit,
talking and carrying two grocery bags, a purse, with
her sunglasses on the top of her head.* SHE *puts one
bag down on the Up* L. *dining table. Ocean sound
drifts out as* ELLEN *speaks.*)

ELLEN. Stay where you are. It's just me. Sorry. John
and I automatically always ring three times just to let
each other know we're home. And now the habit is so
engrained—(ELLEN *takes the other grocery bag into the
kitchen and back to the deck.*) If you want to know
about peculiar, you should have come to the hardware
store with me. Nothing. Not a single car. Oh, listen. On
the news in the market they had on about (SHE *points
upstairs.*) Said it was a suicide attempt over the baby.
(*Has unwrapped and now puts out ashtrays on the two
tables and in the living room.*) I'm sure if you keep talking, Ellen, someone will answer you. (*Then answering
herself.*) Don't be too sure. Oh, oh. And I know you
want the good news about the fire. It's worse. But it's
contained. Which means—(SHE *stops because* FLORRIE
*abruptly stands up, having gathered her things, and
goes to the now open sliding glass door.*) Florrie? May I
get you anything?
    FLORRIE. A gun? (FLORRIE *exits feeling around
perimeter of glass door with the shoes* SHE *is carrying to
be certain it's open into the living room where* SHE *then
collects her tatting.*)
    ELLEN. Okay. No more talking. I'll let you—oh, but
the policeman at the store said the other side of the
highway should be open very, very soon. He said the
trucks have got just about—

FLORRIE. (*Appearing in the doorway.*) Forgive me for interrupting. May I ask one question?

ELLEN. Absolutely. As long as it's not about the book. Nothing about the book until everybody finishes it.

FLORRIE. I wanted to ask about the highway being opened. I never, ever, want to discuss the book. But I would like to get out of here. As fast as I can.

ELLEN. Well, I hope at some point we can talk about the book. But they *are* clearing the other side of the highway very fast, he said. And it's all over the radio, so even though the phones are out, the kids will know you're okay. This is just something you learn to live with in California . . .

FLORRIE. Is that right? Well, thank you so much for educating me. And please—let me know the second the traffic is moving. The very—second. (*Crosses Up into living room to get her belongings.*)

ARNOLD. Florrie? How much of it have *you* got left?

FLORRIE. About, I don't know, three chapters. But I can give you my review right now.

ELLEN. I just ask you not to form an opinion until everyone's finished.

FLORRIE. (*As* SHE *passes the living room door* SHE *stops.*) I can give you my opinion in one word. (FLORRIE *turns and exits Off* L. ARNOLD, *carrying the book, proceeds onto the deck and crosses towards* ELLEN *still at the table.*)

ARNOLD. I bet the word is "swell." I'm most crazy about page thirty. (*Reads.*) "Lionel could be sweet. Lionel could be kind. Lionel could be generous. He could be. But he wasn't."

ELLEN. Everything I tried to prevent from happening is happening.

ARNOLD. (*Reading.*)"It was a posh and elegant dinner

party. Lionel's wife was working and couldn't attend. Lionel suddenly noticed his wife had become the topic of conversation and he was about to chime in when a guest said, 'Whatever happened to that silly nobody she was married to?' 'I'm right here,' Lionel said. There was a tense and embarrassing pause and the guest said, 'Oh. Well, whatever happened to you?'" See, the impressions we never know we make until someone tells us.

ELLEN. Oh now, Lionel (HE *glares at her.*) — I mean, Arnold. You're thinking "she's hurt me." And I (*Pointing to her ear.*) am hearing that and thinking, "I haven't hurt him." And now you're thinking, "She's trying to get out of this." And I am thinking, "oh, God, now he's thinking I am trying to get out of this." So let's just say out loud what we are thinking.

ARNOLD. You just did. Do you want to hear my fav?

ELLEN. No.

ARNOLD. Right here. (*Reads.*) "When his wife worked it was as though Lionel didn't exist. Over breakfast one of those mornings suddenly Lionel looked over at her and said, 'Did I hurt you last night making love?' 'Why would you say a thing like that?' she responded. 'Because you moved,' he said." I've always said if you're going to dish it out, you have to take it. And I can take it.

ELLEN. And I can dish it out, huh? Oh, Arnold, the book is filled with old jokes, old stories, lines — but they're used to make a whole new point. Like the characters all *seem* to be one thing but I make it very clear they're not.

ARNOLD. Well, now that I know what I seem to be, let me go find out what I am. (*Starts to leave. Turns around.*) You little dickens. (*He resumes his seat in the living room.*

ELLEN *goes back to work with an attempt at "keeping busy means keeping sane."*

During this we have been watching MAE *coming down the stairs and go into the kitchen where* SHE *puts down a cup and saucer* SHE *has carried down.* SHE *also carries "the book" and her and* FLORRIE'S *robes. Although* SHE *is all dressed now,* SHE *still has the rollers in her hair.*

MAE. Goofy upstairs finished everything. She is up there in your bed reading and crying. Ellen, honey, is this thing open? (SHE *then crosses around to the open sliding glass door taking tiny steps, moving sideways and feeling with one hand to guarantee the door is open, talking all the time* SHE *is doing this.*) I feel like Patty Duke in "The Miracle Worker." (*Puts robes down on chair* L. *and crosses below the chair.*) Oh, Ellen, honey, did I love your book. But I have no idea who I am.

ELLEN. You loved the book?

MAE. It's wonderful. Now who am I?

ELLEN. Did you finish it?

MAE. Yes. Who am I?

ELLEN. Mae, I'm so glad you like the book!

MAE. Honey, I love the book, but would you please explain to me why John didn't read any of this when you were writing it?

ELLEN. Because he said if he did people would say he helped me write it.

MAE. Believe me no one's ever going to say he helped you write this.

ELLEN. He is not the husband in the book, Mae. It was never my intention to make him the husband in the book.

MAE. I think the road to hell is paved with those very intentions. I never intended to get involved with the Christian Scientist next door. In fact, he was very involved with another lady. All I remember him telling me about her was that she was a Christian Scientist too, and that she was very, very short. I don't know why I remembered those two things, but I did. Anyway, one night I had this dream. I dreamed that I was at this raucous party in a Christian Science Reading Room. And there he was sitting on the couch with this lady. Well my heart stopped. I got so upset that she'd see us smile or look at each other and misunderstand it or something, that I didn't know what to do and I just stood there frozen. And then they both got up and I saw that she only came up to his knees. That woman was short as a duck. And then I saw she had no legs. Just this little bitty body with the two feet attached. And I said to myself, 'well he'll never leave her. She hasn't got a leg to stand on.' And I told him my dream the next day and I thought that man would just fall apart. And the next thing I knew we were out together every night. Until it started getting serious and I started getting guilty. I mean it hasn't been that long I've been alone.

ELLEN. Mae, haven't you figured out that your husband would be the first person to want you to be married again?

MAE. You know what I did just figure out? People like us make things too damn complicated! Don't have the brains I was born with. I'm going back to New York and I'm going to marry that Christian Scientist as fast as I can. Just pray God he doesn't have something desperately wrong with him that he won't admit to and drops dead before I get there.

ELLEN. (*Laughing hard.*) Oh, Mae. (*Phone rings.*

ARNOLD *moves to doorway to listen.*)

ELLEN. Oh, grab it fast, the phones are working.

MAE. (*Picks up phone from under bar and moves it to table Down* L.) Hello. (*Pause.*) Who?

ELLEN. That's not John, it it?

MAE. (*Shakes her head "no", but* SHE *is having difficulty hearing.* ELLEN *takes robes Upstage* R. *and exits through gate.*) I'm sorry, but I can't understand a thing you're saying. (*Pause.*) Sally, it's Arnold's wife, so hang up. Hang up, okay, honey? (*Turns and calls to* AR-NOLD, *covering mouthpiece but* HE *is already on his way to phone.*) Arnold, it's your wife.

ARNOLD. (*On phone.*) Hello. Oh, thank God it's you.

MAE. (MAE, *calls to* ELLEN, *and crosses and stands behind chair* R.) Nutsy upstairs kept talking the same time she was. (ARNOLD *sits on table.*)

(ELLEN *enters, crosses, and stands behind sofa* R.)

MAE. Oh, honey, I wish it had been John too.

ELLEN. Mae, I think the only way I'll ever see John is if he comes by to pick up his basketball. I don't think he's ever going to talk to me again.

MAE. After today he may have to stand in line not to talk to you.

ARNOLD. (*On phone.*) You'll have to talk louder, honey. I can't hear.

(FLORRIE, *now dressed, has come down the Upstage stairs and* SHE *comes into the kitchen and picks up the phone in there and speaks into it.* SHE *has her book, her hair still in curlers, her anger still enormous.*)

FLORRIE. (*Into phone.*) Arnold. Arnold. I would like

to call my family to tell them everything is fine. Which will be the first lie I've ever told them . . . No, the second. I told them I was visiting a friend today.

ARNOLD. (*Into phone.*) Hold on one second will you, darling? (*Holding phone* HE *crosses Up to* FLORRIE *in kitchen window but speaks into phone.*) Florrie, if you've got something mean to say about someone go write a book. (ELLEN *sighs audibly.*)

FLORRIE. (*Into phone.*) I'd appreciate it if you'd let me know if you ever hang up.

ELLEN. Florrie? Florrie, would you like something to eat?

(FLORRIE *glares at her, hangs up phone and exits to the living room and crosses Upstage of chair* L.)

ARNOLD. (*Having crossed back to table* L. HE *sits. Into phone.*) Go on honey, go on. It's like being with the Jukes family around here.

MAE. No one's eaten. People tend to get upset when they're hungry. Or when someone writes a book about them. (*Goes back to searching through* ELLEN's *book.* ELLEN *in kitchen, fixes two plates with food.*)

ARNOLD. (*On phone.*) Well, of course. From what you say we've been stabbed in the back by our own director. And he was our ace in the hole. (*Pause.*) No, I said "ace in the hole" but yours is more accurate.

ELLEN. (*Enters with one plate and gives it to* MAE *and goes back to kitchen to get other plate.*) It may not be a surprise but it's still fantastic.

ARNOLD. (*On phone.*) You want "my news" after that? Oh, please, my news is I've read Ellen's book, I've been caught in a landslide, I've been caught in a fire, I've witnessed a suicide attempt, and which do you think was worse? (*Pause.*) How did you know? (ELLEN *has come onto the deck with the plate handing it to* ARNOLD. *To* ELLEN.) Betty says "hello." (*On phone.*) What? That's the same suicide. (*To* ELLEN.) It's on the news about Sally's suicide attempt. (*Back into phone.*) No, no, no. I was talking to Ellen. Oh, God, no. Be glad you're not here. (*To* ELLEN, *who is exiting toward kitchen and stops, covering phone.*) Now I didn't mean that nastily. You know we're all having a wonderful time. (*Stands.*) Is there another phone I can talk on?

FLORRIE. There is if you want to walk home.

ARNOLD. Ellen?

ELLEN. In the kitchen. (*Exits to kitchen.*)

ARNOLD. (*Into phone.*) Oh, of course. Hold on, honey. (HE *addresses* FLORRIE *while crossing to kitchen.*) I'm going to take this in the kitchen. This is urgent. She's been frantic.

FLORRIE. You want to see "frantic" you stay on that phone.

ARNOLD. (*Exiting.*) I won't be thirty seconds.

FLORRIE. (*Calling to him.*) I know you won't. (FLORRIE *throughout keeps her eyes on him, her watch and her address book.* SHE *takes out brush, comb and bandana to hold rollers after looking through her address book.*) My kids are at their grandmother's who for eighteen years has lived out here at the same number and I still don't know it.

ARNOLD. Would you please hang up that other phone. Thank you. (*To* FLORRIE *as* ELLEN *who enters from kitchen hangs up the phone.*) Florrie, I get another thirty seconds because I couldn't even hear. (HE *slides the window shut and begins talking on the kitchen phone.*)

MAE. Florrie, it's on the radio about Cuckoo-nunu upstairs. Now don't worry, *you* weren't mentioned.

FLORRIE. (*Working with hair still.*) Then we know who didn't write that report.

ELLEN. (*Finally.*) You're just furious at me, Florrie, and if you're wondering if I'm getting it, yes.

FLORRIE. (*Starts, then a decision not to speak on it. Still formal, still cold. Moving her bandana, rollers, brushes for hair to the coffee table, sitting on sofa R.*) Does anyone mind if I brush out here? I'm feeling too nervous sitting in the tinderbox with the fire.

ELLEN. Of course not.

FLORRIE. (*Not looking at her.*) Thank you very much.

MAE. Mine's dry too, I think. (*FLORRIE, now the total hairdresser, crosses to MAE, feels MAE's head front and back . . . then.*)

FLORRIE. Take out the rollers, and I'll comb you out. (*It is obvious SHE was a professional hairdresser and still is as SHE crosses back and sits on sofa R. and works with her own hair.*) Has she let it drop when this book is coming out?

ELLEN. (*Between sofa and chair L.*) I know absolutely if you had taken the book home and read it in a quiet and non-chaotic atmosphere the way I planned, whatever is going on with you would not be going on. Next week. (*Crosses back to kitchen window counter cleaning up.*)

MAE. May I ask a question?

ELLEN. Not about the book. Not until they finish.

FLORRIE. Don't wait for *me* to finish.

MAE. It's not about the book. It's about the title. Why "The Supporting Cast"?

ELLEN. (*Surprised.*) Because everybody in the book is related to somebody famous. That's the *subject* of the book. Well, *you* got that didn't you, Florrie?

FLORRIE. Yes, Ellen. You probably should sit down to hear this, but I did finish high school.

MAE. (*To* FLORRIE.) I mean to you is this a title that sells?

FLORRIE. Ask her why she didn't call it "The Losers."

ELLEN. Because they're not, Florrie. In fact, they're the very reasons the successful people are successful. (*From the counter* SHE *brings down silver coffee pot, creamer and sugar on a tray and sets it on coffee table and remains there.*)

FLORRIE. In at least one case however they are not the reason.

MAE. I still have no idea who I am.

ELLEN. I told you before, Mae, no one's anyone. Everyone is a composite. (*Crosses to counter to get cups and saucers.*)

FLORRIE. Oh, come on. Do you mean to say Lionel in that book is not your friend, Arnold there?

ELLEN. (*Crosses between sofa and chair* L.) See, this is exactly what I don't want. When you all finish then we'll talk.

MAE. (*To* FLORRIE.) The only composite Cleo is is a composite of everything you say and do.

FLORRIE. (*Toward* ELLEN.) I hate Cleo. (*Toward* MAE.) And so must the person who wrote her.

ELLEN. Cleo is my favorite character.

FLORRIE. (*Openly angry now.*) She is dumb.

ELLEN. She's innocent.

FLORRIE. Anyone that innocent is dumb.

ELLEN. She lives only for her family, Florrie. Holding that family together and making it work is what she is and what she does.

MAE. (*Exasperated.*) Who the hell am I?

ELLEN. Mae, no one is anyone. I keep telling you. (*Crosses to counter to get cups and saucers.* FLORRIE *has moved hair supplies and tatting bag from coffee table to small table* R.)

FLORRIE. (*Begins brushing* MAE'S *hair almost violently.*) I don't know who you are either, Mae, or I'd tell you. I do know you're much too likeable and intelligent to be Cleo.

ARNOLD. (*Slides open the kitchen window holding a dead phone in his hand, yelling.*) Florrie? Did you do something to this phone?

FLORRIE. (*Yelling back, still doing* MAE'S *hair.*) I didn't get a chance. Some selfish man was hogging it.

ELLEN. (*Crosses to sofa* R. *and sits to pour coffee for them.*) It's probably out of order again, Florrie.

FLORRIE. (*Furious. Mocking.*) Ellen, you're kidding. I wondered what it was. You mean when a person doesn't hear anybody on the other end, the phone is out of order? Oh, thank you for explaining it. (MAE *leans forward to get cup of coffee.*) Mae, sit. (FLORRIE *pulls* MAE *down by her hair and then styles it, wrapping and fashioning it.*)

ARNOLD. (*Agitated, hurries around, entering the deck. From time to time* HE *will go to the phone, lifting it to see if it's operating again.*) Well, that director has ruined us. He's done everything the exact opposite of what he promised. And why? Who can guess? Try and guess?

FLORRIE. He's having a nervous breakdown.

ARNOLD. Worse. He's having an affair.

ELLEN. With who?

ARNOLD. I'm not supposed to say.

ELLEN. Betty?

ARNOLD. Our star.

MAE. Betty is having an affair with your star?

ARNOLD. (*Crosses between sofa and chair* R., *exasperated.*) No, I'm having an affair with the star, Betty is having an affair with four stage hands, I don't know what the hell you're all talking about. (*Crosses* L. *to phone and tries it.*)

ELLEN. Arnold, clearly something's happened to our brains.

FLORRIE. *I* take that as a compliment.

ARNOLD. (*At phone table* L. ARNOLD *lifts phone and puts it down again.*) I just want to get out of here. We're like hostages. (*Moves back to the bar.*)

ELLEN. Arnold, you're going to get yourself so upset.

ARNOLD. (*Crosses between sofa and chair* L.) I'm already upset. From now on my wife says *I* produce or *she* doesn't write. I mean, please, I've never produced.

ELLEN. Oh, Arnold haven't you learned yet that no one knows anything. We're all faking it.

ARNOLD. I'm not at all sure I'm the producer *type.*

ELLEN. You know how you become a producer, Arnold? You say "I'm a producer."

ARNOLD. Alright, you want to know the truth under the truth? Honestly? I am too afraid I'll fail and fall apart. (*Crosses Up* C. *in front of glass door.*)

MAE. I don't believe what I'm hearing.

ARNOLD. I'm much better behind the scenes.

MAE. That's Lionel right from the book.

ELLEN. (*Trying to stop her.*) Coffee, Mae? Have some coffee.

FLORRIE. (*Crosses Up* C. *to* ARNOLD.) How the hell you ever turned out to be this terrific Lionel is beyond me.

ARNOLD. I find it very accurate. And I find yours very accurate too. (*With two hands he pulls his mouth wide and wiggles his tongue like an idiot making noises. Then crosses Downstage* C. *towards phone while* FLORRIE *turns and glares at* ELLEN, *then* SHE *crosses Up* L. *behind large dining table.*)

MAE. What Arnold just said is right out of Ellen's book.

ELLEN. (*Urging her plate on her.*) Mae, you didn't eat. Here, eat.

(FLORRIE *crosses behind the bar.*)

MAE. (*Taking plate. To* ARNOLD.) It's just identical to what you're talking about. Just identical. You'll see when you get to the next to last chapter where Lionel gets to take over, fails all over the place, starts sobbing in front of everybody, and has to be taken home by his wife in a cab. (*Silence.*) You two should have taken Evelyn Wood.

ARNOLD. (*Crosses into the living room and sits on the sofa there with the book.*) Let me see that.

ELLEN. (*Crosses into living room after* ARNOLD.) Oh no. See, this is bad timing now. Arnold, I hope you don't misread that. (ARNOLD *waves her away and* ELLEN *comes into doorway and speaks to the* OTHERS.) Now you see that is not Arnold. I mean it's not like that ever happened. That never happened. It's something I imagined. It's just that you are the only friends I have who are related to famous people. But you know what this is like? Like photographs. Like when people love those silly, dull, flattering pictures of themselves, that look nothing like them. When the pictures with the hair mussed up or no makeup or the goofy expression that you hate at first, well those are the ones that you ultimately come to treasure. You do. Absolutely. Those silly, exaggerated ones. Ultimately. (*Crosses to* FLORRIE *at the bar.*) See, this is the very reason I wanted to hand each of you the book, let you take it home, explain—

ARNOLD. (*Suddenly* HE *enters Up* C. *in doorway.*)

This is cruel. This is beyond cruel. I have never been cruel to you, you bitch! (*Slams the book on the floor.*)

ELLEN. (*Crosses Up C. to pick up the book.*) Arnold, stop it. Now let's everyone stop it. I didn't just write *you*. Was that exactly *you*?

ARNOLD. That you would imagine that of me. A putz. So sniveling and small. To see me so childish. (HE *stamps his feet, almost crying and crosses back into the living room.*)

ELLEN. It's just that Mae related what you just said to what's in the book. You know, life imitating art.

ARNOLD. (*Interrupting, crossing back into doorway, taking book from her.*) Art! Art! Did you hear her call this ca-ca art? (*Slams book on floor.*)

ELLEN. (*Picks up book.*) I don't know why I said "art."

ARNOLD. Pornography. Pornography you should have said. (*Takes book from her again and throws it on the floor.*)

ELLEN. (*Picking book up.*) Arnold, it's not you so shut up. (*Puts book on dining table.*)

FLORRIE. *You* shut up. What happens to Cleo? Do we find out the reason she's so stupid is because she's had a lobotomy?

ELLEN. Cleo is wonderful.

FLORRIE. Cleo is a retard.

ARNOLD. I hope your house *does* burn down with you in it.

ELLEN. (*Crosses behind sofa L., yelling.*) It is very hard to see the picture when you're standing inside the frame.

FLORRIE. Oh, cut the crap. (*Picks up book from dining table.*) Oh, wait till my husband reads this. Oh, brother, is he going to love me in this. Did he pay you to write it? You have me so dumb in this book people will probably come up to me on the street and say "Okay, real fast, spell 'Mom' backwards." (*Crosses to bar and slams book down on counter.*)

MAE. (*Crossing Downstage L., goes around chair L. and stands above the chair.*) Ellen, I can see that you've got your hands full, but I'm not Kitty. You're Kitty, right?

ELLEN. There is much of me in Kitty, yes.

MAE. Well the only other woman in the book is Dee-Dee.

ELLEN. (*Exasperated.*) Dee-Dee is Sally. I mean — I didn't mean that. Dee-Dee is just very vaguely based on Sally. In fact, Dee-Dee isn't Sally at all.

ARNOLD. Except where she jumps naked into the fountain at Lincoln Center.

MAE. Who else is there? If you invited me here I must be in there, right?

ELLEN. Mae? Who is the kindest, sweetest, most dear character in the book?

FLORRIE. We know who it's not.

MAE. The one I like the most it the writer's father. (*Pause. Waits. Then.*) I'm the writer's father?

ELLEN. It's a composite.

MAE. (*Pause. Then turns to the* OTHERS.) Do I seem butch to people?

ELLEN. Oh, please, everyone, will you please. You're my best friends.

FLORRIE. (*Interrupting, yelling.*) Your friends? Your friends? How stupid do you think I am?

ARNOLD. Did that bitch say "friends"? (*Lifting the book.*) You know what you have done? You have ruined my life.

ELLEN. (*Taking book from him.*) Arnold. I love you

very much and I love Lionel in the book very much. Ultimately this is a very positive book.

ARNOLD. Oh "positive" your nose. (*Crosses Up in front of glass door.*)

FLORRIE. (*Gets book out of her purse next to chair L. and crosses back to bar.*) If this rotten thing is positive then I am not only stupid I'm begging to be committed. (*Going through the book fast.* SHE *has many, many little pieces of paper, marking places, sticking out of it.*) Wait a minute. Wait, wait, wait. I've marked it. Because I may be dumb but I'm smart enough to afford a good lawyer.

ELLEN. Florrie, *you're* the one who's being cruel. I wrote you because I love you.

FLORRIE. (*Found a spot.*) Oh, who could doubt it? Listen to this. (*Reads.*) "So many people referred to her as 'poor Cleo' that many people came to believe 'poor' was actually her first name." (*To* ELLEN.) Thanks for letting me know. (*Crosses to chair Down R. as* SHE *goes through the book for more quotes, sitting in Down R. chair.*)

ELLEN. I made that up. I made most of it up. That's what a writer does.

FLORRIE. (*Reading, interrupting.*) "Cleo was newly married and decided to surprise her husband with a family-type Sunday brunch. She became the afternoon's hilarity, however, for when her mother-in-law called to tell her she was bringing the bagels, Cleo set two extra places." (*Crosses to* ELLEN.) Did you make that up? (*Crosses back and sits, back to book.*) Did you make this up? (*Reading.*) "She came to pick up her children and stood in the school-ground waiting for the lunch hour bell—"

ELLEN. (*Interrupting.*) Alright, that's enough.

FLORRIE. (*Reading.*) "She was twenty minutes early and was so grateful for the solitude. She sat on the bench and watched the classroom windows. She hadn't even noticed that the old derelict had sat down next to her."

ELLEN. Give me that book.

FLORRIE. (*Reading.*) "She tried to remember that once she had sat in school rooms like those. Simple rooms and simple times. The derelict had begun to sing and to sway and Cleo decided to stay there in her own quiet circle of reflection."

ELLEN. Okay, that's enough.

FLORRIE. (*Reading.*) "And in a moment she found she was singing and swaying along with the derelict and smiling and happy and young."

ELLEN. I want you to knock this off, Florrie.

FLORRIE. (*Reading.*) "They finished the song together and Cleo turned to the derelict and smiled. And he smiled back. She felt so warm and tender in the moment. Then the derelict leaned forward and said, 'I suppose a fuck would be out of the question.'" (*To* ELLEN.) I will never tell you another thing as long as I live. Wait, there's more. (FLORIE *hunts for next section to read.*)

ELLEN. I want that book back and I am going to get it. (ELLEN *runs to* FLORRIE *to stop her and in trying to grab the book begins a struggle that takes the* TWO *of them down to the floor.* ELLEN's *trying to get the book and* FLORRIE's *trying to keep it away.* MAE, *alarmed, crosses over to them.*)

ARNOLD. (*To* ELLEN *and* FLORRIE *on the floor.*) Ladies, ladies. Look what I'm calling ladies.

MAE. (*Reaching out.*) Listen, why don't you give *me* the book. (MAE *gets ahold of the book and* FLORRIE *grabs her arm and pulls her down on the floor where now* MAE *is rolling around and caught up in this struggle for the book.* ARNOLD *stands in shock, watching.*)

ARNOLD. My God, it's like mud wrestlers.

(ELLEN *wrenches the book away from* FLORRIE, *and panting hard* SHE *pulls away from them and stands separately Upstage between chair* R. *and sofa.*)

ELLEN. (*Crosses Upstage above sofa and chair.*) Thank you, Florrie. I just want to run out there and throw myself in that ocean.

ARNOLD. It's been done.

ELLEN. What I did is show the world what a remarkable person you are.

FLORRIE. (*Yelling, still on the floor.*) What you did is make me ridiculous. I'm not too stupid to see that.

ELLEN. I did not.

ARNOLD. Are you going to try and tell me that what you did to me isn't vicious?

ELLEN. Yes! I never made anyone here ridiculous and I was never vicious.

FLORRIE. (*Grabbing for the book. Yelling.*) Do you want me to show you more how ridiculous you made me?

ELLEN. (*Pulling away with book. Yelling back.*) No! (FLORRIE *sits in chair* R.)

ARNOLD. Oh please, please. It is so violent around here. Like the South Bronx.

ELLEN. Those characters are very exaggerated, very distorted, very heightened . . . (ELLEN *crosses*

Downstage L. *to bar and wipes her face and hands with cloth there.*)

ARNOLD. (*Interrupting. Shouting.*) They're very betrayed by their very good friend is what they are. Oh my God, how can we stop this book?

FLORRIE. Wait a minute. Those waivers there. What happens if we don't sign those waivers there?

MAE. (*Crossing to bar and signing hers.*) Well, I'm signing mine right here and now. Where are they, Ellen?

ELLEN. They're right here, and if you don't all sign the book won't come out.

ARNOLD. If she fakes my signature I want everyone here to witness I never signed. Never, never signed. Never. Never.

FLORRIE. Then there is no way this so-called book is ever coming out.

MAE. (*Loud, crosses next to* ELLEN *at bar, putting her arm around her.*) It seems to me you should both be excited just to be in a book. How many people before put you in a book?

ARNOLD. Listen, she comes off like a saint. You were so good and holy in the book nobody knew it was you.

FLORRIE. If you want to talk about holy, what about 'Kitty' there. (*Pointing to* ELLEN.)

MAE. (*Crosses to* ARNOLD.) I never would have know Lionel was *you* either. (*Slight pause.*) I found him a fabulous person.

ARNOLD. (*Sarcasticaslly.*) Oh, thank you. (*Looks to the* OTHERS.) Unbelievable. Why are we even talking about it. The book is not coming out. (*To* FLORRIE.) Right? (ARNOLD *sits on sofa* R.)

ELLEN. Lionel *is* a fabulous person. *Cleo* is a fabulous person. The book is *about* fabulous people. Finish it.

FLORRIE. Cleo is the living link to the apes.

ARNOLD. I promise you if we did not stop it this book would someday take its proper place in history right next to the sneak attack on Pearl Harbor.

ELLEN. Nobody understands.

FLORRIE. I understand. I understand, Ellen, how the letters fit together and make words and the words make sentences and I can even figure out what those sentences mean and I hate it, and I hate that I am in it, and most of all I hate that you view me as a cretin.

ARNOLD. Is a cretin worse than a horse's ass?

FLORRIE. And thank God I can stop it.

MAE. (*To* ARNOLD.) Pardon me, before I heard you say how accurate it was.

ARNOLD. Oh, please.

MAE. (*Crosses to doorway* C.) I am now going upstairs and check on the loony-bag. My only regret is if they ever do the movie, Spencer Tracy is not alive to play me. (MAE *turns and exits upstairs.* ELLEN *sits on small Down* L. *phone table.*)

FLORRIE. (FLORRIE *is tatting and trying to concentrate on it.*) You want to know what your rotten book is? What it honest to God is? It's everything I ever feared anybody ever thought of me. Oh pul-eeze, I know what I'm like. I've even been unfortunate enough to have to see it. One night, at one of those premieres, you know how they show those things on TV later? Well there I was with all the elite—chewing gum. I was the only person, out of all of them, wearing glasses. Guess who had this big button undone and the different colored brassiere strap hanging out? Maybe that's why I can't get a sign. That sign that he cares. Why should he care. (*Gathers up her knitting.*) You want to know why your book hurts so much? Because it's right. (*Gets up to exit.*)

ELLEN. Florrie, I never meant to hurt you.

FLORRIE. (*Interrupting, turning back from living room.*) But I guarantee you one thing. I swear my pig-headed, impossible husband is probably the only performer in the world who wherever he wakes up, in whatever city, in whatever country, he's got his kids, he's got his wife, right there. And when that infuriating, immature, spoiled brat of a husband and I fight it's right in the center of the living room where the kids, the friends, the gas man, anyone is welcome to hear. (*Starts to exit and turns back again.*) And there is not a Sunday morning in that conceited slob's life that he doesn't wake up to his whole family in bed with him, laughing and jumping and loving that stupid jerk.

ELLEN. Florrie, I thought that is what I wrote. You're a fabulous human being.

FLORRIE. I know I'm a fabulous human being. But you make me a half-wit in your book. (FLORRIE *crosses Upstage sofa* R. ELLEN *turns away frustrated.*)

ARNOLD. At least you don't fall apart at success. At least you don't have a wife who sits smiling in some cab because you fell apart.

ELLEN. (*Crosses to sofa* L.) Arnold. Lionel took over to show her that all by himself he's important, but he didn't believe it. (*Kneels.*) That's why he fell apart. She's smiling in the cab because even if he doesn't believe in himself he has a wife who believes in him.

ARNOLD. (HE *gets up and crosses to the bar, stopping to lift phone for a second, then sits.*) Were you planning to add thousands of footnotes to explain all these things?

ELLEN. (*Standing. Yelling.*) It's all there, Arnold. That's what the book's about. It's about half the world.

FLORRIE. When your own husband, who is to me a saint of a man, finished it and moved out, did that not tell you anything at all?

ELLEN. Florrie, that is very painful to me.

FLORRIE. Oh?

ELLEN. And I don't want to discuss John.

FLORRIE. Oh?

ARNOLD. It's a little late not to discuss John. Chapters six, seven, and eight tell you more than you ever want to know. *I'd* move out on six alone.

ELLEN. That character is not John. That character is a symbol. For all the successful people in the world who do not appreciate the people who help make them successful.

FLORRIE. Is Cleo a symbol for all the out-patients in the world?

ARNOLD. Ah, I just got it. That's why we saw John at the Beverly Hills Hotel last night. He's living there.

ELLEN. (*To* FLORRIE.) "No" to you. (*To* ARNOLD.) And "yes" to you. (*Exasperated,* ELLEN *crosses behind sofa as* FLORRIE *crosses to* ARNOLD *at bar.*)

FLORRIE. He probably moved out because he thought he was Cleo. (*Goes behind bar and* ARNOLD *sits on phone table.* ELLEN *crosses Downstage in front of sofa.*)

ARNOLD. I hope he's happy with the way his bed is made.

ELLEN. Will you tell me something? Will you both please tell me something? Because I feel like I'm going crazy. I mean didn't either of you see that you don't have to go on living your life in somebody else's shadow? Didn't you see how you don't have to stand behind somebody ever again? You can stand right next to them? (*Pause.*) Oh. You didn't get it.

FLORRIE. (*Crosses to* ELLEN *in front of sofa.*) Wait a minute "didn't get it." *I'm* not your dumb one who didn't get it. I get it. You're the one who doesn't get it. You don't get that you just lost your husband, lost you friends . . . and when that lunatic upstairs finds out what you did to her you'll probably lose your life. (*Moves between sofa and chair* L.)

ARNOLD. (*Crosses to* ELLEN.) I suggest you hide anything sharp.

FLORRIE. I suggest you just hide.

ARNOLD. All I hope is that those two sex scenes of hers are made up. (ELLEN *turns and stares at him. A pause.*) (*To* FLORRIE, *then looking around panicked.*) Oh my God.

FLORRIE. I don't know what I did in my life that God protected me from telling you more.

ELLEN. I guess I cannot climb inside your heads so I don't know how I can make you understand. It's just so frustrating.

FLORRIE. (*Crosses to chair* L.) You want to know what's frustrating. To hear *that* poop when we all know the only reason you wrote this trash was to make a bundle.

ARNOLD. Listen, I can hear what you must have said to yourself. "If I can make them happy by listening to their secrets, their fears, their woes, wonderful. And if I can make a million bucks doing it then *I* can be happy too."

ELLEN. (*Very angry.*) Now wait a minute. Just wait one minute, you two. I can understand you're surprised. I can even see how you might be confused. But I could never understand it if you two believed I actually did this for money.

FLORRIE. Perish the thought. I thought you did it to save the world and all mankind.

ARNOLD. And think how much more you'll make than Judas.

(ELLEN *lets out a groan of frustration and stays there in front of chair Downstage* R.)

MAE. (*Entering out on the upper deck, urgently calling.*) Psst, psst. Ellen, she's been balling her eyes out and we've had a very nice chat. She is on her way down and I thought you'd want to know. And Ellen, she has a lot she wants to say to you.

(*Mae exits. During the above* SALLY *has come down the stairs and through the living room and* ELLEN, FLORRIE *and* ARNOLD *turn and see her coming.*
SALLY *is inching her way through the sliding glass door space, not trusting the door is actually open.* SHE *has her face turned away, her arms flailing.*)
(MAE *will hurry through the living room and enter the deck during this and cross to bar, pick up a waiver and a pen and cross over to* SALLY.)

SALLY. (*Crosses in front of sofa.*) Ellen. Ellen, Ellen, Ellen. (*Clutches the book to her breasts.*)

ELLEN. (*Uncomfortable.*) Sally?

SALLY. (*To the* OTHERS.) Have any of you read it?

FLORRIE. Most of it.

SALLY. I have never been so upset.

ARNOLD. It has that effect.

SALLY. I haven't cried that much since — "The Thorn Birds."

ELLEN. "The Thorn Birds."

SALLY. I wailed.

MAE. See, she liked it.

ELLEN. She liked it?

MAE. Liked it a lot. Sally'll sign your waiver. Ask her.

SALLY. Oh, I'll sign anything you want. Where? Give it to me. Anything. (MAE *gives her waiver and pen and* SALLY *signs it and hands paper to* ELLEN, *touching her.*)

It is a privilege to even touch this hand. An honor. (*Spotting* ARNOLD SHE *starts cooing, crossing to him Downstage* L., *taking his lighted cigarette from him.*) Oh, Arnold, I knew you were still here. Even upstairs I could smell the smoke. You were Lionel. I understand you so much better now. (*Smiles patronizingly and shakes her head.* ARNOLD *gives* ELLEN *a hard stare.*) Florrie was Cleo. (*Touches* FLORRIE *and laughs as* SHE *crosses back to* ELLEN.) All those wonderful contradictions.

MAE. And she got me like that. (*Snaps her fingers.*)

SALLY. (*Next to* ELLEN.) Oh, yes, Mae. Ellen, that was — genius is what that was. It was so clear she was the writer's father. All I kept thinking was if they ever do the movie what a shame Spencer Tracy is dead. (*Takes* MAE'S *hand and kisses it.*)

ELLEN. (*Takes a plate from coffee table to window sill.*) Then you understand it's just bits and pieces, a composite. I mean it's not — an expose or anything.

ARNOLD. (*Not buying it.*) It's closer to a documentary.

SALLY. It's the invention I marvel at. To bring them all to *my* house. (*Throws a kiss to* ELLEN *and circles chair* R. *before ultimately sitting in it.*)

FLORRIE. What?

SALLY. I suppose that you made me the lead so you could see them all through fresh eyes.

ARNOLD. Wait a minute. Wait a minute. Who did you think you were?

SALLY. (*Turning. Surprised.*) Kitty, of course.

ELLEN. Kitty?

ARNOLD. Kitty?

MAE. Kitty. Kitty. Right. I thought you'd be as fascinated as I was by Sally's . . . understanding of the book.

SALLY. (*Sits on Down* R. *chair.*) And it is worth the

whole book to get to that last chapter. (SALLY *throws* ELLEN *a kiss.* ELLEN *crosses to coffee table and moves coffee things to kitchen window ledge and* SHE *remains there.*)

ELLEN. Yes, well they haven't all read the last chapter yet.

SALLY. (*Covering mouth, interrupting.*) Oh. Then I shouldn't say anything. But that's the whole book right there. You'll die.

FLORRIE. I bet.

SALLY. I read the last chapter twice. But then I took Evelyn Wood. (*Crosses to them.*) See, all the famous people are invited to a testimonial without their partners. And I—I mean, Kitty, invites the partners over and we end up having this testimonial of our own where everybody tells everything about themselves and what they think of their husbands and wives and the humor stops. And you see exactly who they are and what they are. Look. Goose bumps. (SALLY *crosses back to chair* R. *and stands.* ARNOLD *and* FLORRIE *grab for their copies and* HE *sits on small phone table and* FLORRIE *goes behind bar as* THEY *hurriedly skim the last chapter.*) Oh, Ellen. it is so moving. No. It is more than that. It's profound. (*Throws kiss to* ELLEN.)

MAE. And say what you told me about Dee-Dee.

SALLY. Oh, yes. See, I thought Ellen was much too hard on herself there. Oh, but you know what I loved? I loved the jumping into the fountain at Lincoln Center. (*Laughs hysterically as* SHE *says.*) That sounds like something *I* would do. (*Points to* ELLEN.) *And* I admire revealing how under the whole facade of "healthy Ellen," you admit how screwed up you really are. I've been that way, and I can identify. (SHE *sits in the chair Down* R.)

ELLEN. Sally, I just—first of all I'm very glad you're

alright. (SALLY *throws* ELLEN *a kiss.*) But you have to know that incident and you have been all over the news all afternoon. (*Sits on Downstage arm of Down* L. *chair.*)

SALLY. What did they say?

ELLEN. It's that all the newsmen were around covering the fire and they picked up on it. Because of who you are.

SALLY. What did they say?

ELLEN. They said that you reacted to the news of the baby by trying to commit suicide.

SALLY. Oh, thank God. I was so afraid they were going to tell I was just drunk and stoned.

ELLEN. Sally, I think it might have been better if they had. They completely misunderstood.

SALLY. Ellen, don't be silly. Suicide has so much more dignity than plain drunk. Imagine getting so stupefied drunk that you trip and fall in the ocean . . . and are too stoned to find your way out.

ARNOLD. Are you telling us that was not a suicide attempt?

SALLY. Oh, Arnold, please, I never go anywhere unless I've studied the travel folders. Now please, sweet Arnold, please. Let's let this secret bind us all together. It's very important to me. And there's another reason. Actually I had the idea before I read Ellen's book, but I know you'll all never believe that now. Anyway, I want to write a book of my own. My own autobiography. And a thing like that suicide thing can make you a best seller before you even write it. God, what I wouldn't give for a picture of me being dragged out of that ocean for the cover. Well, do you know what we could do? Maybe we'll go out there someday and fake one. Because a thing like that is an "event." I learned that from politics. Once you get in the news for an "event" everybody wants to know everything about you.

ARNOLD. Incredible.

SALLY. Isn't it?

ELLEN. Arnold, shush.

ARNOLD. Don't 'shush' me. It's incredible.

ELLEN. (*Stands between sofa and chair Down* L.) I just know you wouldn't have refused to sign those waivers or have been this upset if you could see the point I was making. It's an enormous and important point that the whole would needs to know.

SALLY. (*Stands.*) Who wouldn't sign? And how could anyone here be upset when all of you in the book are exactly the way you are in life?

FLORRIE.   ARNOLD.
Oh, is that right?   The way you are in life maybe.

ELLEN. Florrie . . . Arnold . . .

SALLY. I know. I know. Ellen is tough and hard on these people because she's showing how they work, work, work for somebody else and they have no idea the value that they have themselves.

MAE. This is what I've been hearing about upstairs.

SALLY. Until I read the book I thought all of you had no value either. But now I see that you're not as unimportant as you seem. (SALLY *puts out cigarette in ashtray on cocktail table.*)

ARNOLD. You are as crazy in the book as you are in life.

ELLEN. Arnold, please, I will handle this, Arnold. Just not right now.

ARNOLD. Oh, no, no, no. This is your game and you are cheating. (*Turning to* SALLY.) You are Dee-Dee! You are the one who *has* and who *is* the loosest screw in the book. (ELLEN *sits in chair Down* L.)

SALLY. Oh, how funny. Your saying that. (*Laughs.*

Then more laughter. Then roars with laughter as SHE
crosses to ARNOLD *and pinches his cheek. Continuing
laughing* SHE *hugs* MAE. *Laughing still* SHE *goes to*
ELLEN *who is sitting in the chair Down* L. *and the
laughter stops fast as* SALLY *falls on* ELLEN *covering her
as* SHE *starts to choke her. Quickly,* FLORRIE *and* MAE
pull SALLY *off, but even while being dragged away,* SAL-
LY *is trying to grab at* ELLEN. ARNOLD *stands behind
sofa. As* THEY *seat her in chair* R. *and hold her down*
MAE *is* R. *of chair,* FLORRIE *is* L. *of chair.*)That's just the
one I didn't want to *be.*

ELLEN. Sally, have you lost your mind? Stop this
nonsense at once. Now stop it!

SALLY. My oldest, my best friend. The person I came
to for my life.

MAE. Now she didn't *mean* to be malicious. She just
was.

SALLY. You are the most dangerous, evil, cruel
monster.

ARNOLD. Quiet. Quiet. Now let's all calm down, so we
can plan how we can kill ourselves.

SALLY. What? What have you done to me? (*Throws
head dramatically to the Downstage side.*)

ELLEN. I promise you it will never happen again.

SALLY. Again? I trusted you.

ELLEN. (*To* SALLY.) What I am is sorry.

SALLY. What I am is sorry too.

ELLEN. So sorry.

SALLY. So am I. Sorry. (SHE *smiles and throws* ELLEN
a kiss. SHE *is released and crosses to* ELLEN, *saying
"sorry, so sorry, sorry" and when* SHE *reaches her chair*
SHE *leaps on her and starts strangling her again.*) Sorry
I ever met you. (MAE *and* FLORRIE *pull her off, drag her
back to the chair Down* R. *where* MAE *sits on her lap and*

FLORRIE *stands behind the chair holding her.*)

ELLEN. (*Stands between chair and small table* L.) I don't know how what was so good up here got so misunderstood there. (*Pointing to book, moves Up* C. *between couch and chair Down* L.) But it did and I'm stunned. I never, never meant to say you people are ridiculous or foolish. What I was trying to say was these people are the backbones of the world. You never, ever hear about them yet there they are supporting half the world. Who stops to think *ever* that half the world is nurturing, caring and providing so the other half can make it big? And people get it. Other people get it. If you had only *heard* the people who bought the English rights, the French rights, the German rights. (*Straightening chair pillows that came off in the struggle as* SHE *continues.*) I mean if you just stop and think. There is the other half out there making the money, getting the praise, being admired. Who admires what we do? So this book is about *us*. Not (*Pointing to each one.*) you, you, you, you, but *us*. *All* of *us*. And you know what I learned writing this book? I mean the point of the whole thing? The point I can't stand that you're not getting? (*Picks plates up off of dining table and crosses to* C. *doorway with them.*) You're not just my friends and people I love and people I find so valuable, you're heroes. Goddam it, you're heroes. (ELLEN, *very emotional, exits to kitchen with the plates. A moment. Then* ARNOLD, MAE *and* SALLY *go into the kitchen after* ELLEN. *When* THEY *arrive there is a pause. Then.*)

ARNOLD. The English rights, the French rights, the German rights?

MAE. What are you talking about with the "rights"?

ELLEN. (*Pours a glass of water.*) What? Oh. Just . . .

the subsidiary rights.

MAE. You're kidding. Already?

ARNOLD. Before it even comes out you sold the foreign rights?

ELLEN. (*Enters living room and crosses behind the bar.* THEY *follow* ELLEN, *standing above the table.*) Yes. The Scandinavian, the Far Eastern, the South American. Oh, I can't remember them all. And the paperback rights have set a new record.

ARNOLD. So if you've set a new record this book is a hit before it even comes out?

ELLEN. I'm only quoting my publisher. He says it's a gigantic hit. It begins next week as a Book-of-the-Month alternate.

FLORRIE. (*Who hasn't moved.*) You've got to be kidding.

SALLY. I'm so sad it's only an alternate.

MAE. I'm real impressed.

ARNOLD. How can you not be impressed? It's awesome.

ELLEN. See, you would have been the famous ones. I have to go on these book tours and talk shows all over the country, all over the world, just talking about *you*.

MAE. (*Slight pause. Then.*) Would you like a picture of me dressed as the writer's father?

SALLY. Oh, I should get my hair cut if you're going to want pictures. Because this could be unbeatable publicity for *my* book.

ELLEN. I'd love to have pictures if you don't mind.

SALLY. Mind? This might get me on those game shows and panel things.

ARNOLD. (*Crossing to bar and signing his waiver.*) Would you want any of us to appear on those talk shows with you? To say like "I'm Lionel in the book."

ELLEN. I'd be thrilled. I'd be honored.

ARNOLD. Well, I'll think of some more crazy things. And my diet starts this second. (*Gives paper to* ELLEN *and crosses and sits on sofa* L.)

MAE. Uh, I may pass on the talk shows. Would it be crazy if I signed autographs in bookstores.

ELLEN. Oh Mae, it is so sweet of you to think of that.

FLORRIE. (*The hold-out. Having watched from* ONE *to the* OTHER *coldly as* THEY *gushed.*) I wonder why *you* didn't think of it. You seem to have thought of everything else.

ELLEN. (*A moment.* SHE *knows* FLORRIE *is the tough nut to crack.*) Florrie. Oh, Florrie. How will they ever find anyone to play you in the movie? (SALLY *squeals.*)

MAE. A movie?

ARNOLD. I'm fainting.

ELLEN. Didn't I say that first? Oh, that's the thrilling part. The movie sold right from the galleys. (*Crosses and stands behind* L. *corner of sofa.*)

FLORRIE. (*Crosses Down to* ELLEN, *slowly.*) What kind of actors are going to play *us*?

ELLEN. Big stars. Big, big stars.

FLORRIE. (*Cannot suppress the wild delight. Crosses to bar and signs waiver.*) My husband will kill himself.

ARNOLD. Who's going to play *me*? Should I get an agent?

FLORRIE. Now he'll be referred to as *my* husband. (*Gives paper to* ELLEN.)

ELLEN. (*To* ARNOLD.) Who do you want?

FLORRIE. See if I can play myself.

SALLY. Oh, me too.

MAE. It's more than thrilling. It's a fantasy almost. They'll probably follow it up with "Gone With The

Mae." "Mae of Arabia," "Mae and the Seven Dwarfs."
(FLORRIE, *crossing Up of sofa, laughs and gives* ARNOLD
a pat.)

ELLEN. You'll be celebrated. Everywhere. Forever.
It's—

SALLY. (*Interrupting, laughing heartily as* SHE *crosses
Stage* L.) Oh, Ellen, I'm just thinking of how jealous
and guilty he's going to be when he hears I'm *in* one
book and writing *another*. (*Sits on Downstage arm of
chair Downstage* L. *laughing.*)

ELLEN. Sally, excuse me. This is none of my business.
But I sure as hell hope very soon you come off all that. I
hope you call up that poor slob and let him go. And not
only for *his* sake, but for yours. (*Doorbell rings.* ELLEN
becomes upset.) Now who—Oh. I hope we're not being
evacuated. (ELLEN *starts to exit. Doorbell. Three rings.*
ELLEN *stops. Turns upset.* FLORRIE, *back at her tatting
sits in chair* R.) That's John. Three rings is—(*Starts to
go. Turns back.*) But stand by to evacuate just in case.
(ELLEN *exits.* SALLY *sits in deep thought.*)

FLORRIE. What should we do? Go stand in the ocean?

ARNOLD. They talk about New York while people in
Los Angeles are living lives of terror.

MAE. (*Gets up, crosses into living room, gets purse,
and comes back down and sits again.*) Should we try to
save anything?

ARNOLD. Yes. Ourselves.

FLORRIE. I think the reason so many people live in Los
Angeles is because it's so hard getting an apartment in
New York.

SALLY. (*We have watched her decide this, and* SHE

now crosses to phone table Downstage L.) Ellen is absolutely right. Absolutely right. Absolutely. Oh God, I hope it's working. (*Lifts phone, listens, then dials.*) It's working. I've been punishing myself to punish him and that's the end of it. Oh God, what I wouldn't give for a joint right now. (*Startled. Into phone.*) Congressman Stern, please. (*Pause.*) Mrs. Stern. (*Covers mouthpiece.*) That is guaranteed not to reach him. (*Suddenly, stunned.*) George. Oh, George. (*Pause.*) Yes, I heard your news and it doesn't matter. I said that it doesn't matter. No, George, I'm not just being nice. You know that's something I never tried to be. George, let me say this. Just file for the divorce and give me whatever you think is fair. (*Pause.*) Well, George, that's more than fair. (*Pause.*) I just wanted you to know that what was on the news about me was a mistake. (*Pause.*) Oh, George, I *believe* you're in a meeting. Please go back. And thank you for taking the call. (*Pause.*) Oh, George, please don't feel any guilt. (*Pause.*) No, don't feel any guilt. (*Pause.*) Please, George, don't feel any guilt. (*Pause. Hangs up. Looks at them.*) I forgot. He lives on guilt.

(ELLEN *enters.*)

ELLEN. Florrie, Florrie— (ELLEN *to Upstage* L. *corner of sofa.*)

SALLY. (*Crossing Upstage to* ELLEN, *interrupting.*) Ellen. Ellen, I called him. Is it over? Is that all it is? After all that time. (SHE *hugs* ELLEN. *Pause.*) Well, he was fair. I mean "everything," that's fair. (SHE *sits in chair* L.)

ELLEN. (*Suddenly remembering.*) Oh, Florrie, it was for you. It's your husband.

FLORRIE. (*Jumping up, facing her. Hysterical.*) It's what?

ELLEN. That's—that's who was at the door. It wasn't John.

FLORRIE. (*Grabbing her heart.*) Well, what is it? What's wrong?

ELLEN. No, nothing's wrong. When he heard about the fire and he couldn't reach you on the phone he just shut down the set and came out to get you.

FLORRIE. (*Running into living room.*) Where is he? Is he crazy? Where is he?

ELLEN. No, no, no. He was very excited. He said he wanted to get some close-up pictures of the fire. I told him to come back, ring the bell three times and then he wants to pick you up.

FLORRIE. (*Crossing back to her chair.*) See, he's like a little kid. Taking pictures. Oh, God, what a scare.

ELLEN. He's got to get right back so he wants you to be ready. (ELLEN *exits to kitchen.*)

FLORRIE. (*Sits in chair* R.) Is he a pistol? Well, it's a sign. It's a pathetic sign, but it's a sign.

ELLEN. (*Entering with a cheesecake on platter.*) I forgot all about Miss Grimble's cheesecake.

(*As* SHE *heads for the dining table* L., *a slow rumbling starts and increases and increases and* EVERYONE *stops and shakes and jiggles and hangs on as the whole stage vibrates with an enormous rumbling noise and the furniture moves and hanging object sway and some things crash to the floor.* MAE *holds her breasts from shaking. Lights go up and down. Then it stops.*)

ELLEN. (*Continued.*) (*Holding up the cheesecake then putting it down.*) The cheesecake's right over here if anybody's interested.

ARNOLD. Cheesecake? What the hell was that?

ELLEN. (*Cutting the cake.*) A tremor.

SALLY. (*Shouting.*) Tremor. That was an earthquake. We're lucky to be alive.

(ELLEN *goes behind bar and gets fallen plant, puts it on kitchen window ledge.*)

FLORRIE. I think I peed my pants.

ELLEN. Do you know I never mind them. We always think of that as everything settling into its proper place.

MAE. Oh, let me write that down.

SALLY. Why does everything have to happen to me?

MAE. I wish to hell I hadn't given away all of my Valium.

ELLEN. That wasn't even a big one.

ARNOLD. The entire house almost came down.

ELLEN. (*With a cake knife and plates, about to serve pieces.*) Oh, that wasn't even a big one. That was — (*Suddenly it happens again, interrupting* ELLEN, *who holds the trembling knife and plates. Much rattling and vibrating.* MAE *grabs her vibrating breasts again. Then the shaking stops.*) (*Finishing her sentence.*) That was a medium big one. (*Puts pieces of cake on plates.*)

MAE. (*Crosses Upstage behind sofa.*) You're so helpless. Where do you go?

ELLEN. Actually you're supposed to stand inside a doorway.

(SALLY *rushes to the doorway and supports herself with a hand on each door frame.*)

ARNOLD. (*Crosses Downstage* R. *toward beach.*) *You* go stand inside a doorway. And the whole ceiling will come down on your head. Not to mention the door.

SALLY. And I especially don't want to die now. Not before I finish my book.

ELLEN. Wait now. Hold on. That wasn't an earthquake. That was just an aftershock.

ARNOLD. Oh, is that all it was. (*Rolling down sleeves, fixing tie, getting ready to leave.*)

FLORRIE. (*Crosses* R. *to* MAE.) All I want is ten minutes for my husband to see me famous. Then I'll gladly die.

ELLEN. (*Crosses Upstage* R. *to* MAE.) How different is it from the subway going under you at 59th and Lexington?

MAE. Ellen, you're losing you marbles. One is a natural event and the other is a catastrophe.

ELLEN. And which is which? (MAE *crosses in front of* ELLEN *to the bar where* SHE *pours a drink.*)

MAE. If only the tidal wave could just hold off till tomorrow.

ELLEN. Oh, Mae, there's not going to be a tidal wave.

MAE. From your mouth to God's ear.

FLORRIE. Mae, stay with us tonight. It's much better. No water and we have all these trees around so I pretend it's Connecticut.

ELLEN. Mae's staying right here. Everything is back to normal.

SALLY. Back to normal? When has anything around here been normal? I have been held up at knife point in New York City and I find it was just silly compared to this. I have to go.

ELLEN. Oh no, no, no. Don't go now. The traffic's going to be moving so slowly.

SALLY. As long as it's moving. (SHE *exits into living room and disappears Offstage* L.)

ARNOLD. (*Having crossed Downstage* L. *and clicking the phone.*) Oh, now it is not working again. I don't know why you bother having a phone. I've got to reach my wife. She's going to be hysterical.

ELLEN. Arnold, they'll be very fine very fast. (ELLEN *crosses Upstage* C. *to doorway.*)

ARNOLD. Well, I won't. Florrie, you don't have to pay me that money you owe me for the backgammon if you let me ride home with you.

FLORRIE. (*Hurrying. Putting tatting away.*) Of course, Arnold, of course. I wasn't going to pay you anyway.

SALLY. (*Hearing him in the next room and running in calling him and crossing Downstage* L.) Arnold, Arnold, Arnold, you know I have my rented car. You could ride back with me.

(ARNOLD *hurridly crosses Upstage to living room to get briefcase, countering* SALLY'S *move.*)

ARNOLD. (*Entering from living room.*) Oh, I'd give anything if I could ride back with you. Anything. (*Taking his copy of the book, turns to* SALLY.) But I have decided to stop smoking and you'd get me hooked like that. Goodbye Ellen. Florrie, I'll see you outside. (*Gives cigarette package to* ELLEN, *having kissed her. Starts to leave. Turns back.*) Oh, Goodbye, ladies. After spending the day with the four of you I wonder why women are fighting for equal rights. It would be such a step down. (HE *gives them a final look then exits through the living room and Offstage* L.)

SALLY. (*Gets book from cocktail table.*) Goodbye, Florrie. (*Goes up and hugs* ELLEN, *taking the cigarettes.*) Goodbye, Ellen. (*Waves.*) Goodbye, Mae. Thanks for the drugs. Oh, I hate driving alone out here.

More drivers give me the finger than you would see in a window display of wedding rings. (SALLY *exits.*)

FLORRIE. (*Hurrying, getting her things together.*) Ellen, I'm very impressed that you wrote a book. And I'm very impressed with me to be in it. And you know what else impresses me? You pulled this off, you brat. (*Doorbell rings three times.*) Here I go. Pavlov's dog.

ELLEN. That's your husband, Florrie.

FLORRIE. (*Crosses to* MAE *at bar and hugs her.*) That's the gentleman. I'm surprised he didn't just toot the horn. (*Crosses to* ELLEN *Upstage* C. *at door.*) Wait'll I drop on him we got a new celebrity in the family.

ELLEN. You were always the celebrity in that family. And don't you forget it. (FLORRIE *starts to exit. Stops.*)

FLORRIE. Next time I see you I'll tell you why you shouldn't leave your John out of your sight. Ever. I'll tell you right now. Who wouldn't want him?

ELLEN. (*Hugging* FLORRIE.) Goodbye, Florrie. You're so wonderful.

FLORRIE. (*Exiting, turns back.*) Yeah, well, if you put me in your next book bring my I.Q. up to seventy. (*Exits.*)

ELLEN. (*As* ELLEN *slides the glass door closed.*) New Yorkers are so funny. Because New York is so busy and exciting and interesting that they think they're so busy and exciting and interesting. Then they get out here and they get frightened that they're not, so they blame us. Oh, now, Mae. You know I didn't mean you.

MAE. Oh, I know, I know. You meant a composite. (*Looking at the opening page of the book.*) Did you write the same thing in all of ours?

ELLEN. Yes.

MAE. (*Reading, crosses below chair* L.) "Life is a battlefield which has its heroes; the obscure heroes sometimes greater than the illustrious heroes."

ELLEN. That's paraphrased Victor Hugo. (*Sits on sofa, while* MAE *gets her pen out of her purse.*)

MAE. Do you suppose Mrs. Hugo helped him with that? You know what I want? I want you to write above "To Mae, the writer's father."

ELLEN. Oh, Mae. (ELLEN *laughs and* MAE *hands her pen and book.* ELLEN *starts to write, and the doorbell rings three times.*)(*Starting to exit.*) Oh, that's Florrie. She forgot something.

MAE. (*Stopping her by exiting first.*) Oh, sit down, sit down. I'll get it. You write.

(MAE *slides open door and exits and sitting again* ELLEN *writes in the book. Finishes.*

SHE *is alone and* SHE *is sad.* SHE *takes off her shoes and starts dejectedly cleaning things up.*

A moment passes and a very furtive and excited MAE *appears, entering through the gate Stage* R., *signaling someone to stay right where they are, out of sight.*

ELLEN almost *catches* MAE *signaling as* SHE *turns and sees her.*)

ELLEN. What was it?

MAE. (*Flushed, trying not to act too excited.* SHE *comes out on the deck, crossing Downstage* R. *of sofa.*) Oh. It was very good news. The fire's out and both sides of the road are open.

ELLEN. That is good news.

MAE. I'll help you with this. (*Lifts tray and moves to the window ledge.*) I bet John will hear the news, get real worried and drive out here to see that you're alright.

ELLEN. No. I'm sure he won't.

MAE. (*Crosses back sofa Upstage* R.) I'll bet you dinner in New York.

ELLEN. You're on.

MAE. Ellen, what's John supposed to say to people who think he's the husband in the book? (*Opens book, holding it in front of her.*)

ELLEN. Oh, Mae, anyone who knows John would know he is not the husband in the book.

MAE. (*Closes book.*) Absolutely, now you just make sure he understands that.

ELLEN. Mae, can I tell you something personal?

MAE. (*A look back at the fence.*) No.

ELLEN. John has only been gone 24 hours and I have never missed anyone so much in my life. (*Ocean sound starts blending in again.*)

MAE. You're going to owe me that dinner in New York. Now I'm going upstairs. I've got a surprise for you. For your book. Your first award. (MAE *hurries, exiting, running up the stairs and out of sight.*)

ELLEN. (*Crosses Up to glass door, calling to* MAE.) Oh, Mae. I don't want an award. I just want to *deserve* an award. (SHE *shuts the sliding glass door and walks Downstage* L. *in thought, then to herself.*) The only award I want right now is — (*And the sound of a basketball bouncing Offstage* R. *stops* ELLEN. SHE *turns to look and sees a basketball go through the hoop.* MAE *appears on upper balcony, watching.*) (*Finishing her sentence.*) Is that.

(*Another basket and* ELLEN *literally runs across the deck, through the gate and Offstage* R., *and we hear* JOHN *and* ELLEN *laugh and see only their feet under the fence as* THEY *undoubtedly kiss. As that occurs,* MAE, *anxious to witness the reunion, has run down the steps, through the living room and right into the glass door and goes to the floor as* —)

CURTAIN

PROPERTY PLOT

Bar (built in)
Two arm chairs
Sofa
Round table
Small table
Sofa pillows
Deck chairs
Deck table
Pillows
Coffee table
Ferns
Plants
Table setting for five
Five napkins
Tablecloth or place mats (five)
Sunglasses (Sally)
Football jersey
Hockey stick
One sneaker
Plants (kitchen)
Watering can
Air conditioner
Purse (Sally)
Tray
Three water glasses
Pitcher
Lip-gloss (Sally)
Basketball
Suntan lotion
Food in kitchen
Towel
Aspirin
Valium

Mirror (Sally)
Watch (Sally)
Sunglasses (Ellen)
Kleenex
Purse (Ida)
Ice bucket
Wine glass
Ice
Bowl with lemon wedges
Phone
Vodka
Tomato juice
Tabasco
Lea and Perrin sauce
Horse radish
Appointment book (Ida)
Eye glasses (Ida)
Vase with rose
Tray
Tatting bag (Florrie)
Yarn
Tatting needles
Two glasses
Cigs. (Arnold)
Lighter (Arnold)
Ashtrays
Lunch food
Candles
Matches
Salad
Salad dressing
Five dishes
Silver serving dishes
Serving carts

Silver trays
Pizza
Dr. Brown's celery tonic
Pastrami
Sturgeon
Fancy salads
Lox
Herring
Chicker livers
Coffee
Silver coffee server
Five coffee cups
Saccharin in silver container
Five books "The Supporting Cast" by Ellen
Tonic
Blankets (2)
Coffee in coffee pot
One of "Ellen's" books wet
Robes (Ida & Florrie)

PROP PLOT "THE SUPPORTING CAST"

ACT I
Kitchen:
  Above sink two glasses of water
  Right of sink pitcher half full of Bloody Mary's
  Downstage Shelf:
    Silver tray with fake food and several pieces of real
      food covered with towel
    Tray with pizza covered with towel & pot holders
    Large round tray with fake food covered with towel
    Bottle of wine
    Wine glass
  Upstage Shelf:
    U.S. Stove:
      Coffee pot
      Cup and saucer
    D.S. Stove:
      Bowl of peanuts
      Cutting board with parsley
      Bowl of salad with spoon and fork
  Onstage Shelf:
    Five white plates
    Five blue napkins
    Five knives
    Five forks
    Five spoons
    Pot of daisies with removable ones
    Bowl of lemons
Down Left:
  Bookcase:
    Top Shelf:
      Stirer

        Brown glass with celery stalks
        Can of open tomato juice
        Box of kleenex
        Towel
        Knife
        Can opener
      Second Shelf:
        Three towels
        Tray
Right of Bookcase:
  Bar:
      Ice bucket with ice
      Bottle of wine
      Bottle of scotch
      Bottle of vodka
      Bottle of perrier
      Pitcher of water
      Water glass
      Old fashioned glass
      Bottle opener on string
      Towel
    Top Shelf:
      Horse radish
      Tabasco
      Lea and perrin sauce
      Wine glass
      Aspirin bottle with aspirin
      Eight yellow glasses
      Four brown glasses
      Pen
      Old fashioned glass
      Four "Supporting Cast" books
    Bottom Shelf:
      Extra pitcher of Bloody Marys

Two "Supporting Cast" books
Bottle of vodka
Open Shelf:
  Telephone
Behind Bar:
  Wastebasket
Down Right of Bar:
  White table on marks
Center:
  Trick arm chair
Left Center:
  Love seat
Front of Love Seat:
  Coffee table
  On Coffee Table:
    Small saucer
  Behind Coffee Table:
    Basketball
Right of Love Seat:
  Large arm chair
Down Right of Chair:
  White table on marks
Up Right Under Step:
  White beach towel
Off Up Right on Back of Set:
  Two bathrobes
Up Left:
  Round white table
  On table:
    Cruet with oil
    Cruet with vinegar
    Salt shaker
    Pepper shaker
In Living Room:
  Sofa on marks

Coffee table in front of sofa
Chair upstage on marks
Chair downstage on marks
On chair:
  Gray sweater
On Balcony:
  Sneaker
  Football jersey
Off Left:
  Sally's slipper socks
  Arnold's briefcase
  Sally's purse with pills in bottle
  Florrie's purse
  Florrie's address book
  Florrie's knitting in gold bag
  Florrie's book with markers
  Red scarf with two hair pins and several bobby pins
    and hairbrush
  Cup and saucer
  Bag with groceries
  Bag with ashtrays (3), moisterizer
  Pack of cigs. with lighter
  Ellen's purse with sunglasses in it
  Car keys
  Mae's purse with handkerchief on top
  In Purse:
    Compact
    Cigs.
    Lighter
    Pill Bottle w/3 pills
    Handkerchief
    Lipstick
    Glasses on string in case
    Kleenex
    Halls cough drops

    Nail file
Off Right:
   Pack of cigs with lighter
Under Counter in Kitchen:
   Silver tray with three cups and saucers
   Silver pot of coffee
   Cheese cake in tray
   Five small plates
   Five small forks
   Plate with fake food, napkin, fork
   Plate with fake food, napkin, fork, real food

Strike:
   All dirty glasses
   Three trays of food
   Five plates
   Five knives
   Five forks
   Five spoons
   Five napkins
   Two pitchers of Bloody Marys
   Stirer
   Salt
   Pepper
   Two cruets
   Tomato juice
   Lemons
   Salad
   Cushions back
   Coffee table back to marks
   Trick chair back to marks
   Dish from coffee table
   Arnold's briefcase to above chair right in liv. rm.
   Lea and perrin sauce, horseradish, lea & perrin sauce,

    asprin all back to shelf under bar
   Sally's purse off left with shoes
   Florrie's purse and knitting on coffee table
   Mae's purse to coffee table in liv. rm.
   Basketball to prop table

Set:
   Arnold's book on sofa in living room
   Book on coffee table in living room
   Stool in kitchen with book
   Cup and saucer upstairs
   Right back cushion on right arm of sofa
   Book on coffee table
   4 pages from address book on coffee table

Set in Kitchen:
   Tray with cheese cake

Offstage Counter:
   Silver coffee pot
   Tray with cups
   Tray with cream & sugar
   Plate with fake food & napkin
   Plate with fake and real food
   Fork and napkin

On Stage Shelf:
   Five small plates
   Five small forks

Check:
   Two books first shelf under bar
   Pen first shelf under bar
   Four brown glasses under bar

Personal:
   Sally:
     Compact
     Sun glasses
   Arnold:
     Lighter

THE SUPPORTING CAST COSTUME PLOT

Ellen
Act I
  Beige linen jacket
  White wool slacks
  Brown crushed cotton blouse
  White espadrilles
Act II
  Blue oxford cloth shirt
  Light blue jeans
  Straw belt
  Repeat espadrilles
Florrie Cutler
Act I
  Red on cream print shirtwaist
  Raspberry with cream pin stripe silk jacket
  Red leather belt
  Red leather open-toed espadrilles
  Red bead/gold necklace
  Red enamel bracelet and earrings
  Beige teddy
  Green terry robe
  Gold bag
Act II
  Repeat Act I
  Dry duplicate of dress
Mae
Act I
  Navy blue two-piece knit suit
  White with navy trim blouse and tie
  Navy suede shoes
  Navy handbag with hankies
  Pink terry robe

White full slip
Pin watch on jacket
Gold earrings
Act II
Repeat Act I – strike jacket
Dry duplicate
Sally
Act I
Rust print silk dress
Lavender blue cotton jacket
Raspberry silk shawl
High-heeled strap sandals
Amber beads
Drop earrings
Green chiffon hip drape
Bracelets
Act II
Repeat Act I – dry duplicate
Tennis socks
Arnold
Act I
Blue blazer
Blue cotton shirt
Striped tie
White sneakers
Red executive length socks
khaki pants
Act II
Repeat Act I

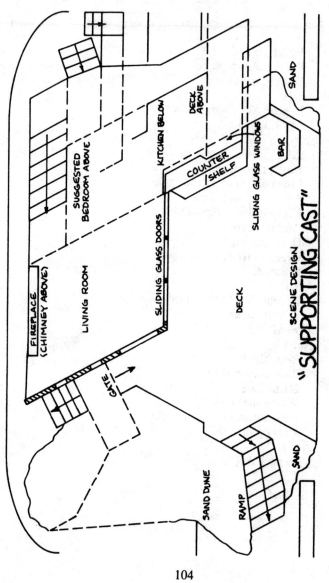

SCENE DESIGN
"SUPPORTING CAST"